Handcuffed

Handcuffed

What Holds Policing Back,
and the Keys to Reform

MALCOLM SPARROW

BROOKINGS INSTITUTION PRESS
Washington, D.C.

Library of Congress Cataloging-in-Publication data are available.

ISBN 978-0-8157-2781-1 (pbk : alk. paper)
ISBN 978-0-8157-2782-8 (epub)
ISBN 978-0-8157-2783-5 (pdf)

9 8 7 6 5 4 3 2 1

Typeset in Adobe Caslon and ITC Officina Sans

Composition by Elliott Beard

Contents

Acknowledgments

This book should properly be regarded as one more product of the Executive Session on Policing and Public Safety, a collaboration between the National Institute of Justice (NIJ) and the Program on Criminal Justice Policy and Management at the Harvard Kennedy School. Over the course of six years, from 2008 to 2014, a group of leading police chiefs and a handful of academics and others met twice yearly to debate the theory and practice of policing, and to see what we could do collectively to advance the development of the profession. The Executive Session generated a total of twenty-three papers, published jointly by Harvard and NIJ, as the New Perspectives in Policing series.

I am grateful to all the members of the Executive Session for their commitment to this process and the extraordinary range of experience and insights that they brought to the table. I won't name them all here, as they are all named on every paper published in the New Perspectives series.

I had the special pleasure of working on the steering committee, whose task was to identify critical themes, plan the Executive

Session meetings, manage the portfolio of papers commissioned to make sure important areas were covered, and act as the editorial board for the papers published. I am particularly grateful to the other members of this steering group—Chris Stone, Thom Feucht, Christine Cole, Darrel Stephens, Anthony Braga, Sean Smoot, Brian Welch, and Brett Chapman—for the many hours of rich and challenging conversations we shared in the course of that work. Through them I felt reconnected with the profession in a way I had not for some fifteen years, and was privileged to benefit from their vast knowledge of the field and collective insight into current developments.

Special thanks to NIJ for granting permission for me to reuse some of the material from the four papers I authored in the New Perspectives series. Thanks also to the American Society of Criminology for permission to include in this volume an adapted version of my paper "Crime Control through a Regulatory Strategy: Joining the Regulatory Fold," which was first published in *Criminology & Public Policy* in May 2012.

Throughout this volume I have cited many of the other New Perspectives papers, drawing particularly heavily from those written by Anthony Braga, Charles Ramsey, and David Sklansky, because these most closely aligned with the core theme of this book—the need to re-examine the foundational ideas of community and problem-oriented policing and to work out what has impeded the development of those ideas over the last twenty-five years and prevented them from reaching maturity.

ONE

Introduction:
The Crisis in Policing

These are tumultuous times for policing in America. Thanks in part to the almost ubiquitous presence of video cameras, the American public has recently had the chance to see the very best and the very worst of police conduct.

At the scene of the Boston Marathon bombings on April 15, 2013, Boston police officers and other emergency workers instinctively ran toward the site of the explosions to help the injured and take control of the scene, even while nobody knew how many more bombs there might be. Video footage made plain to all the classic courage of first responders reacting to a traumatic situation with professional discipline and putting their own lives at risk for the sake of the public they serve.

Three days later, on April 18, MIT patrol officer Sean Collier was shot dead in his patrol car by bombing suspects Dzhokhar and Tamerlan Tsarnaev, who were apparently seeking to acquire weapons and perhaps provoke a major confrontation with police. In an extraordinary display of public appreciation for police officers and the dangers they face on a daily basis, more than 10,000 people attended Officer Collier's funeral.

On April 19 Tamerlan Tsarnaev was killed during a gun battle with police in the streets of Watertown, Massachusetts. He had been shot several times by police and then run over by his brother, who was fleeing in a stolen SUV. One MBTA police officer was shot and nearly died from blood loss. The surviving brother, Dzhokhar Tsarnaev, was found later hiding in a boat in the backyard of a Watertown home and apprehended.

Scores of law enforcement officers from federal, state, and local agencies had flooded into the area and cooperated in the search. When it was all over, local residents—who had voluntarily heeded the police request to "shelter in place"—emerged from their homes, gathered on street corners, and spontaneously applauded as buses full of law enforcement officers passed by.

During that week in April 2013, nobody seemed to have anything but praise for the courageous and selfless way police conducted themselves in the face of those extraordinary dangers.

But 2014 and 2015 brought to public attention a series of incidents, many of them video-recorded on the cellphones of passersby, that appalled the public, astonished many, and raised troubling questions about the quality and nature of policing in America. Several incidents involving the deaths of unarmed black men at the hands of white police officers, albeit in different jurisdictions, came in quick enough succession to be perceived as a pattern and to prompt national debate.

The pattern was pretty much established after two high-profile incidents just three weeks apart: the death of Michael Brown in Ferguson, Missouri, and of Eric Garner in New York City. Public concern over the issues raised drew commentary from the president, led to the establishment of a presidential task force, resulted in investigations of patterns of police conduct by the Department of Justice's Civil Rights Division, and spawned protests against police violence—particularly against minorities—that spread across the nation far beyond the cities directly involved.

As soon as the pattern was established, every subsequent incident where police used force then drew unprecedented levels of public and media scrutiny as the public searched for answers to some very basic questions: Do police regularly abuse their powers and use excessive force? How widespread is such abuse? How much is it targeted on minority and poor communities? Why can police not be held accountable even in those instances when their actions appear patently criminal?

New York City, July 2014

On July 17, 2014, Eric Garner died after being detained in Staten Island by officers of the New York Police Department. His arrest (for selling cigarettes illegally on the street) was captured on video, and appeared to show Garner being held in a chokehold for about fifteen seconds and being brought to the ground. The use of chokeholds contravenes NYPD policy. Once on the ground he complains repeatedly, "I can't breathe," but the video shows no signs of police providing or calling for medical assistance. Garner died shortly afterward, and the New York City Medical Examiner's Office concluded that Garner, who suffered from asthma, died partly as a result of the chokehold. Eric Garner was black, and a father of six.

Ferguson, Missouri, August 2014

On August 9, 2014, Michael Brown, an eighteen-year-old black man, was shot dead in Ferguson, Missouri, by a white police officer, Darren Wilson. This incident was not recorded on video. Brown was unarmed when he was stopped by Wilson. In defense of his own actions, Officer Wilson stated he feared for his own life when Brown reached for his (Officer Wilson's) weapon. Wilson subsequently resigned from the police department. No charges were brought against him as a result of the local investigation into the shooting or as a result of a second investigation conducted by the Department of Justice.

Each of these incidents produced its own curious aftermath. In New York, Mayor Bill de Blasio publicly expressed his concerns about police violence and sympathy for the protesters. He told how he had advised his own biracial son to "take special care" any time he interacted with police, which the police unions interpreted as suggesting police were dangerous and to be feared. The unions lambasted the mayor for failing to support them adequately, and hundreds of NYPD officers later turned their backs on the mayor during the funerals of two NYPD officers ambushed and killed in December 2014.[1]

In the days following the death of Michael Brown, protests in Ferguson turned violent and images of police in riot gear using armored personnel carriers and other military-style equipment fueled public perceptions of police as militaristic, armies of occupation, ruthlessly crushing both protest and criticism in the name of crime control.

Other incidents followed quickly, reinforcing public perception of an alarming pattern.

Cleveland, Ohio, November 2014

On November 22, 2014, a twelve-year-old African American boy, Tamir Rice, was shot dead by police in a city park in Cleveland, Ohio, while playing with a toy gun. Two police officers,

Timothy Loehmann and Frank Garmback, were responding to a public complaint of a "male sitting on a swing and pointing a gun at people." Rice was shot dead by Officer Loehmann within two seconds of the patrol car arriving on the scene. The officers reported that Rice had failed to respond to their shouted warnings, and had "reached toward a gun in his waistband." Multiple witnesses contradicted this account in their grand jury testimony, and video evidence makes clear Rice had no time to react at all to any warnings that might have been given, as he appeared to be shot even before the police car had come to a halt.

Under a rarely used Ohio law, activists and community leaders appealed directly to the Cleveland Municipal Court for the officers to be arrested and indicted. Presiding judge Ronald B. Adrine, having reviewed the video evidence, found probable cause to charge Officer Loehmann with murder and his partner with negligent homicide.[2] Whether the officers will be charged, and with what offenses, depends on the outcome of a grand jury investigation.

North Charleston, South Carolina, April 2015

On April 4, 2015, a black man, Walter Scott, was shot dead by North Charleston police officer Michael Slager following a routine traffic stop for a defective brake light. Scott fled on foot, possibly because he was afraid of going to jail for failing to make child support payments.[3] A video taken by a bystander captured the later stages of the foot pursuit and clearly showed Officer Slager discharging eight rounds from his service weapon as Scott was running away from him. Five of the bullets hit Scott, who died at the scene.

We learn more about the problem of police violence and how it can persist and might be covered up when a video only surfaces after some significant delay. That allows time for the police to provide their account of the incident before the video evidence is available, and possibly before they even know that any video recording exists. In the case of Walter Scott's death, it took more than two days before the video became available to authorities. Feidin Santana, who captured the shooting on his cellphone camera, initially kept quiet about the video, fearing retribution, but was angered when he heard the police account of the incident and made the recording available to Scott's family and to the media.[4]

Presumably Officer Slager, in providing his initial account of the incident, had no idea that any video existed. He claimed that Scott, during a scuffle, reached for the Taser on his (Officer Slager's) belt, and that he (Slager), therefore, felt his own life was in danger. He immediately gave an explanation over the police radio—"Shots fired and the subject is down; he took my Taser"—knowing that such transmissions are recorded, hence, putting his story on the record.[5]

Without the video evidence, that story might well have stood. But the video became public on April 7, showing Slager repeatedly firing at Scott as he ran away, and Slager was arrested within a few hours and charged with murder.

The video of Scott's shooting immediately went viral, of course, along with the revelations about Slager's original and clearly false account. For the general public, the case raises serious concerns about other police incidents not captured on video, where there is little or no objective evidence about what happened, and where officers provide similar justifications for shooting an unarmed person. How often do stories such as Slager's get told? What chance is there that investigations into officer-involved shootings—typically conducted by detectives from the same department (that is, by the involved officer's own colleagues)—will actually establish the truth? How widespread is the practice of lying to conceal police abuse of force?

It would be interesting to know some basic facts and figures. For instance, how many times a year do American police officers shoot unarmed suspects and subsequently justify their actions by claiming they felt their own life was in immediate danger, either because the suspect appeared to be about to pull something out of a pocket or, in the course of a scuffle, the suspect seemed to be reaching for the officer's own weapon? In the absence of witnesses or video evidence or contradictory forensic evidence, such accounts are unlikely to be refuted. Such incidents would normally end up classified as justifiable homicides—or, to use the peculiar language of the police profession, as "good shootings."[6]

The fact of the matter is that we have no idea how often this happens, as the United States does not gather any reliable national statistics on officer-involved shootings, or on other deaths at the hands of police, or on deaths that occur in police custody. Federal databases exist, but submission of those data by law enforcement agencies remains voluntary and is, consequently, acknowledged to be woefully incomplete.[7]

Why can the United States not produce reliable statistics on the number of civilians shot and killed by police? The usual explanations point to the difficulty of categorizing incidents in sufficiently consistent ways to make the figures meaningful, as well as the cost and difficulties involved in gathering data from the roughly 18,000 law enforcement agencies that operate in America. But it seems incongruous that the U.S. federal government manages to report annually and nationwide (through the Uniform Crime Reports) on matters such as burglaries, larcenies, robberies, and sexual assaults—where all the same definitional complexities and data collection difficulties apply—but they cannot do the same when it comes to officer-involved shootings despite the fact that these events are much less numerous, somewhat easier to define, and much more significant.

In an attempt to fill the information vacuum, the *Washington Post* began compiling a database of every fatal shooting by police in 2015, as well as of every officer killed by gunfire in the line of duty. The study focused only on fatal shootings, and, therefore, did not include other deaths at the hands of police, or deaths in police custody, or nonfatal shootings. Even so, the *Post*'s tally as of December 24, 2015, was 965, which equates to roughly 2.7 people shot dead by police, on average, per day.[8] This is more than double the rate revealed by the official statistics compiled at the federal level for previous years. Analysis conducted by the *Washington Post* showed that at least 243 (25 percent) of the 965 shot dead showed signs of mental illness at the time they died at the hands of police.[9]

The *Guardian* newspaper, which also tracked the number of people killed by U.S. police in 2015 (whether by shooting or otherwise), showed a year-end tally of 1,134. According to the *Guardian*'s crowd-sourced information, 1,010 of these deaths were by gunshot. Their analysis also showed black people were killed by police at more than double the rate for whites and Hispanics/Latinos. Of the African Americans killed by police, 25 percent were unarmed, while 17 percent of the whites killed were unarmed.[10]

According to the *Washington Post*'s analysis of 385 police shootings that occurred during the first five months of 2015, officers had been charged in only three cases. Officer Slager in North Charleston was one of these. In all three cases that led to indictments against police officers, video evidence had surfaced that showed officers shooting suspects during or at the end of pursuits on foot.[11]

In a different study using multiyear data, the *Washington Post* examined the rate at which police officers were charged as a result of fatal shootings. They found only fifty-four cases where officers had been charged since 2005, representing a tiny fraction of the thousands of police shooting incidents that had occurred in a decade.[12]

The *Post*'s analysis showed that in most of the cases where prosecutors did press charges the victim was unarmed, and there were also "other factors that made the case exceptional, including: a victim shot in the back, a video recording of the incident, incriminating testimony from other officers, or allegations of a cover-up."[13] According to prosecutors interviewed by the *Post*, to charge a police officer requires "compelling proof that at the time of the shooting the victim posed no threat either to the officer or to bystanders." Absent one of these exceptional factors, it seems generally impossible to disprove officers' claims that they felt themselves endangered. According to Philip Stinson, one of the criminologists working with the *Post* on the study, "To charge an officer in a fatal shooting, it takes something so egregious, so over the top that it cannot be explained in any rational way."[14]

Even where individual killings are justified, the patterns of practice that result in so many deaths can still be alarming. Ronald L. Davis, head of the Department of Justice's Office of Community Oriented Policing Services, told the *Post* reporters, "We have to get beyond what is legal and start focusing on what is preventable. Most [police shootings] are preventable."[15] According to the Department of Justice, "The shooting of unarmed people who pose no threat is disturbingly common."[16]

The President's Task Force on 21st Century Policing, which released its final report in May 2015, addressed the need for reliable data on police use of force and the need to bolster the credibility and independence of investigations into use-of-force incidents. With respect to the gathering of data, the task force noted the existence of voluntary reporting programs on arrest-related and in-custody deaths, but recommended mandating law enforcement agencies to "collect, maintain, and report data to the Federal Government on all officer-involved shootings, whether fatal or nonfatal, as well as any in-custody death."[17]

The task force also recommended mandating "external and independent criminal investigations in cases of police use of force resulting in death, officer-involved shootings resulting in injury or death, and in-custody deaths."[18]

Baltimore, April 2015

On April 12, 2015, Baltimore police arrested Freddie Carlos Gray Jr., a twenty-five-year-old African American man. Gray had run away from police, even though the police did not know why. They gave chase and apprehended him, alleging that he was in possession of an illegal switchblade. The arrest itself was videotaped by bystanders, but did not appear violent. Gray was handcuffed and transported to a police station in a van without being secured by a seatbelt as departmental policy requires. At the end of the trip, Gray was in a coma and was taken to a trauma center. He died on April 19 from spinal cord injuries. Six Baltimore police officers were immediately suspended and have since been criminally charged with various counts relating to Gray's death.

Protests over Gray's death in Baltimore were mostly peaceful, but turned violent the day of his funeral and resulted in millions of dollars' worth of looting, property damage, and destruction within the city. The violence was short-lived, however (partly due to the imposition of a citywide curfew and influx of substantial law-enforcement assistance), and appears in retrospect largely attributable to the coordinated actions of opportunistic high-school kids intent on looting and capitalizing on the unrest. Some of the criminal opportunism seems to have been highly targeted. During the rioting, thirty-seven pharmacies in Baltimore were entered, and oxycodone availability on the streets reached unprecedented levels shortly thereafter.

Baltimore's police commissioner, Anthony Batts, who had been brought in from Oakland in 2012 to reform the Baltimore Police Department, asked the Department of Justice to come in and conduct a systematic review of Baltimore's departmental policies and practices.

The fact that the Department of Justice has the power to examine and intervene in the practices of local police departments is a curious legacy of the videotaped beating of Rodney King by the Los Angeles Police Department in March 1991. The Crime Control and Law Enforcement Act of 1994 contains a provision inserted as a result of the reforming efforts of Representative Henry Waxman of California. This provision makes it illegal to "engage in a pattern or practice of conduct by law enforcement officers [or other officials within the criminal justice system] that deprives persons of rights, privileges, or immunities secured or protected by the Constitution or laws of the United States."[19]

The 1994 act also grants the attorney general of the United States, given reasonable cause to believe that such a violation has occurred, the right to intervene "to obtain appropriate equitable and declaratory relief to eliminate the pattern or practice." Over the last twenty years, this provision has provided the foundation for federal intervention into local policing issues and the imposition of consent decrees on numerous major city police departments, especially when infringements of constitutional rights are alleged. It provides an important opportunity for national values and constitutional rights to be reasserted when local police management conceals patterns of abuse or fails to control officers' conduct, when departmental culture stifles or defeats local reform efforts, or, for that matter, when local leaders completely lose their moral bearings.

Department of Justice Investigation, Ferguson, Missouri

There are occasions, apparently, when local police and city officials have completely lost their moral bearings. The Civil Rights Division of the Department of Justice conducted an investigation into the Ferguson Police Department in the wake of Michael Brown's death and the subsequent decision by a St. Louis County grand jury in November 2014 not to bring charges against Officer Darren Wilson.

The Department of Justice investigation found insufficient evidence to bring civil rights violations against Wilson, but its broader inquiry into the policies and practices of the Ferguson Police Department was absolutely devastating. The publication of a 102-page report on March 4, 2015, led within a few days to the firing of the municipal court clerk and the resignations of the city manager, the municipal court judge, the police chief, and two other police supervisors.[20] The fallout from the inquiry continued with a petition submitted on May 28, 2015, to recall the mayor of Ferguson, which, if it had been successful, would have forced an early mayoral election. The petition was filed by a citizens protest group, Ground Level Support, directly in response to the shooting death and the findings of the federal inquiry. The protest group came twenty-seven valid signatures short of the 1,814 required (15 percent of the city's registered voters) to trigger a recall, and, on that basis, the St. Louis County Board of Election Commissioners ultimately rejected the petition.

The Department of Justice report makes compelling and disturbing reading. It lays bare a policing operation totally focused on the wrong mission and exercising little or no control over the means used to achieve the goals set for that mission.

For observers of American policing (and, in particular, of troubled police departments), the Department of Justice report contains two major surprises. Not so much the racism, corruption, and patterns of excessive force that the federal investigators uncovered. That such phenomena persist in some departments is sad indeed, but no great surprise. The first real surprise is what motivated the Ferguson police staff. For many American police departments, the primary imperative is to show a reduction in reported crime rates. That mission—controlling crime—would strike most members of the public as an appropriate one for any police department to embrace.

What drove the Ferguson police department was revenue raising, a mission that was accomplished through aggressive use of traffic citations and other municipal code violations. Enforcement was often concentrated on minorities and vulnerable segments of the population. According to the report, city officials made maximizing revenue the priority for Ferguson's law enforcement activity, completely distorting the character of the police department:

> Ferguson's law enforcement practices are shaped by the City's focus on revenue rather than by public safety needs. This emphasis on revenue has compromised the institutional character of Ferguson's police department, contributing to a pattern of unconstitutional policing, and has also shaped its municipal court, leading to procedures that raise due process concerns and inflict unnecessary harm on members of the Ferguson community.

City officials exerted constant pressure on police executives to generate more revenue through enforcement, and the pressure was transmitted all the way down through the ranks:

> The importance of focusing on revenue generation is communicated to FPD officers. Ferguson police officers from all ranks told us [federal investigators] that revenue generation is stressed heavily within the police department, and that the

message comes from City leadership. . . . Officer evaluations and promotions depend to an inordinate degree on "productivity," meaning the number of citations issued.

This emphasis dominated the department's approach to law enforcement:

Patrol assignments and schedules are geared toward aggressive enforcement of Ferguson's municipal code, with insufficient thought given to whether enforcement strategies promote public safety or unnecessarily undermine community trust and cooperation.

The focus on revenue also distorted the purpose and values of the municipal court:

Ferguson has allowed its focus on revenue generation to fundamentally compromise the role of Ferguson's municipal court. The municipal court does not act as a neutral arbiter of the law or a check on unlawful police conduct. Instead, the court primarily uses its judicial authority as the means to compel the payment of fines and fees that advance the City's financial interests. This has led to court practices that violate the Fourteenth Amendment's due process and equal protection requirements. The court's practices also impose unnecessary harm, overwhelmingly on African American individuals, and run counter to public safety.

Normally one would expect the court to act as a check on the use of force by police and on the appropriateness of enforcement activities. In Ferguson, however, the municipal court operated as a subunit of the police department. The courtroom itself was physically located within the police station, and court staff reported to the chief of police. The court and police acted in partnership to maximize revenues.

The report describes how a powerful and singular focus on maximizing revenue was accompanied by loose controls on means:

> FPD has communicated to officers not only that they must focus on bringing in revenue, but that the department has little concern with how officers do this. FPD's weak systems of supervision, review, and accountability . . . have sent a potent message to officers that their violations of law and policy will be tolerated, provided that officers continue to be "productive" in making arrests and writing citations. Where officers fail to meet productivity goals, supervisors have been instructed to alter officer assignments or impose discipline.

Officers' violations of law and policy, according to the report, included the following:

- Stopping people without reasonable suspicion
- Using unreasonable force
- Interfering with a member of the public's right to record police activities
- Making enforcement decisions based on an individual's demeanor, language, or expression
- Overreacting to challenges and verbal slights ("contempt of cop" cases)
- Engaging in patterns of excessive force, often during stops or arrests that had no basis in law, and sometimes in ways that were punitive or retaliatory
- Arresting people without probable cause, including instances when they were engaging in protected conduct such as talking back to officers, recording public policing activities, or lawfully protesting perceived injustices
- Arresting people simply for failing to obey officers' orders, when those orders had no legal basis or justification

- Releasing canines on unarmed suspects, without first attempting to use other methods less likely to cause injury
- Using unnecessary force against vulnerable groups such as those with mental illnesses or cognitive disabilities, and juveniles

The report also found evidence of blatant racism expressed in e-mail messages sent through the official e-mail system. Court supervisors and FPD commanders had participated in the exchanges. Investigators found that the burden of oppressive policing was borne disproportionately by African American members of the community, including more than 90 percent of instances involving uses of force.

Of course, such a distorted style of policing could only survive if the department had ways of suppressing complaints and dissent. Federal investigators noted that the Ferguson Police Department frequently failed to respond to public complaints of officer misconduct, that members of the public were often discouraged from lodging complaints, that complaints made were often not recorded, that officers' accounts were automatically believed when in conflict with other witnesses, and that little serious investigation into allegations of abuse took place.

The second striking feature of the Department of Justice report is that the recommendations for the reform of the Ferguson Police Department focus on ideas that have been around for at least thirty-five years! According to the report, getting the Ferguson Police Department back on track would require nothing less than a complete transformation: "Addressing the deeply embedded constitutional deficiencies we found demands an entire reorientation of law enforcement in Ferguson. The City must replace revenue-driven policing with a system grounded in the principles of community policing and police legitimacy, in which people are equally protected and treated with compassion, regardless of race."

The report's recommendation section stresses the implementation of community and problem-oriented policing as the basis for fundamental transformation: the top priority, to "implement a robust system of true community policing," shifting from "policing to raise revenue to policing in partnership with the entire Ferguson community." The report urged the Ferguson Police Department to "develop and put into action a policy and detailed plan for comprehensive implementation of community policing and problem-solving principles" and to "conduct outreach and involve the entire community in developing and implementing this plan."

How could this be, in 2015? The concepts of community-oriented and problem-oriented policing were developed more than thirty years ago, and had become generally accepted by the end of the 1980s as the model for improving policing. These two ideas are simple enough to state, and well known throughout the policing world.

Community policing exploits the power of partnerships, with police and the community working collaboratively to establish priorities within the public safety mission, and working together to deal with the crime problems and other issues nominated as priorities by the community.

Problem-oriented policing, which was championed by Professor Herman Goldstein from the 1960s onward, exploits the power of thought and analysis. Its central tenet is simple: police become more effective if they can identify and deal with the underlying issues that generate crime and other public safety concerns, rather than continuing to respond to individual incidents and violations after the fact and one by one.

Community policing and problem-oriented policing are different ideas, but entirely complementary. There is no conflict between them. Most departments that embrace one end up, quite naturally, embracing the other also.

But what happened to these ideas? How is it that the Department of Justice found it necessary to recommend these ideas in Ferguson, Missouri, roughly thirty years after they had—at least in theory—been adopted as standard doctrine for modern policing?

One explanation might be that these ideas had never reached small-town departments in certain rural areas, and that Ferguson was outside the mainstream and way behind the times. A second explanation might be that the damage to policing in Ferguson was done by the department's dominant performance imperative, with the drive to maximize revenues essentially squeezing out every other dimension of policing quality.

But a third potential explanation is much more disturbing and has much broader ramifications. Maybe these ideas never really took root. Maybe small-town departments, who thought they knew their communities, imagined that they were doing community policing anyway and that implementation was only a challenge for big-city departments.

Perhaps the development of community policing and problem-oriented policing was thrown off track more broadly by other pressures acting on the police profession or by conflicting prescriptions for reform. Maybe these fundamental and potentially transformative concepts never reached maturity. Maybe, in some departments, the organizational culture impeded or defeated the efforts of reform-minded leaders. Perhaps some police departments adopted the rhetoric but failed at implementation, or got stuck in some rut by implementing simplistic substitutes.

The question is important for the entire profession: what happened to community and problem-oriented policing? The Ferguson report certainly raises the question by recommending these ideas as potentially transformative now, in 2015, so long after many in the profession might have assumed they had been completely assimilated into modern police practice. The Ferguson report cannot answer that question, because it is completely and appropriately focused on Ferguson. To probe the issue we would need to look much more broadly across the profession and see what forms the implementation of community and problem-oriented policing have taken and what levels of maturity they have achieved.

Given the current attention to incidents involving the deaths of black men at the hands of police, it might also be useful to see what connection there might be between the specific incidents that occur and the forms or versions of community and problem-oriented policing that the relevant departments had implemented.

New York

New York City, of course, is nothing like Ferguson, Missouri, and their police departments seem poles apart. The New York Police Department has an authorized uniform strength of 34,450 officers, to Ferguson's fifty-four. The NYPD is the largest municipal police force within the United States and has the full range of specialist functions and technical means at its disposal. It has played a prominent role in counterterrorism, and its Intelligence Division and Counter-Terrorism Bureau has officers stationed abroad in eleven different cities.

Representatives of the NYPD, including commissioners, have long been centrally involved in national debates about policing strategy. So it is definitely not the case that the ideas of community and problem-oriented policing could have passed New York by. Indeed, the various leadership teams of the NYPD have embraced the concept of community policing since Ben Ward (commissioner from 1984 to 1989) introduced the idea to the department.

So what similarities might exist between the death of Michael Brown in Ferguson in August 2014 and the death of Eric Garner just three weeks earlier in Staten Island? The two incidents are clearly connected in the public mind, each perceived as part of a larger pattern of police brutality focused disproportionately on minorities. In subsequent demonstrations around the country, protesters used a mixture of placards with the words "I can't breathe" (Eric Garner's repeated complaint before he died), "Hands up; don't shoot" (based on one witness account that Michael Brown was shot while holding his hands up in surrender), and "Black lives matter."

Both incidents involved unarmed black men dying at the hands of the police. Neither Brown's nor Garner's death resulted in the indictment of the officers involved, which, according to poll data, was perceived by nearly all African Americans as an injustice in both cases.[21]

But do these two cases have any more in common than that? What else would the NYPD—the largest of big-city departments in the United States—have in common with Ferguson, which is much more typical of small-town and rural America? Big-city police get much more public scrutiny than their rural counterparts and, thus, might be generally expected to be more restrained and more accountable. The NYPD is certainly regarded in policing circles as a modern and professional policing operation. It has also been the source of several significant innovations in policing, such as the CompStat process, first implemented in New York in 1994 and widely emulated elsewhere throughout the policing world, not just in the United States.

In fact, there are some deeply significant similarities between the NYPD and the Ferguson Police Department. The NYPD, as in Ferguson, is strongly driven by one key performance imperative, powerfully driven from the top of the organization, and producing performance pressures that cascade all the way down through the ranks. The key performance imperative in Ferguson was to maximize revenues from code enforcement. The key performance imperative for the NYPD, since the introduction of CompStat in 1994, has been to reduce the city's crime rate. Specifically, to reduce the *serious* crime rate, with emphasis placed on offenses classified as Part 1 crimes under the Uniform Crime Reporting system.

What the NYPD's CompStat system has done, for roughly twenty years, is place extraordinary pressure on precinct commanders to drive down the crime rates within their precincts. Of course the *reported* serious crime rate might be quite different from the *actual* crime rate, given the fact that a significant proportion of crimes committed are not reported to police. In fact, what NYPD's CompStat system really focuses on is the *recorded* serious crime rate, which—given opportunities for misclassification of crimes and manipulation of statistics—might be much different from the *reported* crime rate.

Strange as it may sound, even though the NYPD and the Ferguson Police Department had settled on quite different central imperatives, the fact that they each had a single central imperative, strongly emphasized and highly quantitative in nature, leads both departments into similarly dangerous waters. A dominant focus on one dimension of performance suppresses other legitimate concerns. A focus on ends, if not matched by effective controls on means, can lead to behaviors that are unwise, risky, or illegal. Officers who perform well in achieving numerical goals may be rewarded or promoted even when the legitimacy or legality of the means they use to get those results is questionable. The organizational culture might even end up making heroes and heroines of those "prepared to do whatever it takes" to hit ambitious targets and make their bosses and organizations look good.

This phenomenon is by no means limited to policing. It has long been recognized within both private sector and public management literature as a potentially corrupting influence, producing organizational deviance of various kinds. Diane Vaughan, who has studied many forms of organizational misconduct, says that trouble arises when the social context puts greater emphasis on achieving the ends than on restricting the means.[22]

Elsewhere I have described and analyzed this class of organizational behavior problems under the label *performance-enhancing risks*.[23] My main concern in writing about them was to stress that, with this dynamic in play, the specific instance of malfeasance that comes to light, however serious, is usually not the real problem. Investigators naturally focus on the specific incident, but that one instance is often just a small clue that there might be a much larger and systematic pattern of abuse, and that we will never affect or transform the behavior of the offending organization until we understand what is really happening inside it, what motivates the improper behaviors, and what mechanisms are being used to shield the improper conduct from outside scrutiny or intervention.

If a police organization applies relentless pressure on its officers to maximize revenues (as in Ferguson), or to lower the recorded crime rate (as in the NYPD), but no counterbalancing controls are imposed on methods, the use of force, fairness in targeting, or integrity in reporting, from the public's perspective the resulting organizational behaviors can be ineffective, inappropriate, and potentially disastrous.

In the NYPD the means to be employed to drive down crime were not left to chance. When the CompStat system was introduced to the NYPD in 1994, the organization specified not only the central goal but also the principal methods to be used within the precincts. "Aggressive street order maintenance" became the order of the day, with street officers demonstrating "zero tolerance" for minor infractions.

The theory—sometimes dubbed Broken Windows policing—was that the imposition of order through attention to minor incivilities and misdemeanors would lead in time to a lowering of the serious crime rate. The label *Broken Windows* stems from research published by Wilson and Kelling in 1982, which showed that visible damage to buildings, if left unattended, tended over time to attract higher rates of criminal damage.[24] Windows left broken and other signs of neglect seemed sufficient to communicate to potential offenders that nobody cared.

There is no convincing research that demonstrates a link between aggressive enforcement of minor offenses and subsequent impact on serious crime rates. So the NYPD's prevailing operational doctrine has been based on a rather tenuous logical extension of the original Broken Windows research. Many scholars are skeptical about the link, and worried that the costs of such an aggressive policing style outweigh the benefits. In commentary offered after the riots in Baltimore, Bruce Western points out important historical parallels and questions the developments of policing strategy in the interim:

In 1967, the National Advisory Commission on Civil Disorders reviewed the events of the previous summer. Detroit, Newark, and over a dozen other cities had struggled with intense episodes of violence and disorder. The disturbances were typically sparked by interactions with police, they began in African American inner-city neighborhoods, and young black men were often in the forefront of the confrontations with police and national guardsmen. . . . Over the next four decades . . . conditions deteriorated in many of America's inner cities even as a new get-tough-on-crime politics—

which included very little compassion—became the national policy and a staple of political wisdom for both parties . . . many cities adopted "quality of life policing," making large numbers of arrests for minor infractions on the theory that this would prevent more serious crime. The research evidence for this theory is mixed at best. Certainly many jurisdictions significantly reduced crime rates without vastly increasing the number of misdemeanor arrests.[25]

If pressed to justify this aggressive, enforcement-centric, zero-tolerance style of policing, the NYPD story is that this is community policing—this is what the community wants; this is what communities are asking the NYPD to provide.

Really? This approach has led to massive numbers of arrests and stop-and-frisk campaigns disproportionately focused within poor minority neighborhoods. It makes enforcement the default answer to almost every problem. Just like officers in Ferguson, NYPD officers are constantly monitored for their enforcement productivity. In New York City, even in 2015, officers' arrests, citations, stops, and other enforcement activities are tallied daily, weekly, and monthly.

The day Eric Garner died, he was selling loose cigarettes on the street, posing no physical threat to anyone. They were "bootlegged" cigarettes, brought into the city without paying the substantial taxes that New York City imposes on cigarettes. Roughly three-quarters of the cigarettes smoked within the city are bootlegged.[26] Nevertheless, selling them on the street is a misdemeanor and, for NYPD officers, arresting Garner would *count*. One more offense recorded; one more arrest made. As it is, Garner died surrounded by NYPD officers, and the video that enraged the public shows rapid escalation of the incident, rough handling, what appeared to many viewers to be the use of a chokehold (which would be contrary to NYPD policy), and a failure to attend to Garner's need for medical attention as he lay gasping for breath on the ground.

The public should be concerned by the incident. But it is important also to delve deeply into the organizational dynamics that underlie the incident. That is precisely what the Department of Justice did in the inquiry into Ferguson and what makes their report so valuable and compelling. Although the inquiry was sparked by the shooting death of Michael Brown, the incident itself is not the focus of their inquiry. Rather, they thoroughly and systematically peel away the layers of the organization, revealing the purposes, culture, beliefs, attitudes, managerial systems, and operational behaviors that constituted the character of policing in Ferguson.

The Purpose of This Book

It would be much better not to have to wait for some tragic incident to occur, for scandals to unfold, for heads to roll, and for public protests to turn into riots. It would be much better for police and public alike to make sure we are clear what style of policing we should expect and how close we are in practice to getting it. We should not have to wait for tragedies to occur before we can address those questions. This volume, like the Ferguson report, aims to look beneath the surface and identify the dynamics and ideas that currently drive policing.

Chapter 2 tackles directly the question of what constitutes success. What are the dimensions of police performance that count? What dangers emerge when a police department allows one specific performance imperative to dominate the agenda? How can balance be restored, and a more rounded sense of service quality developed?

Chapter 3 examines the development of community and

problem-oriented policing and the variety of forms that have emerged. What has prevented them from maturing? What events or conflicting ideas have thrown them off track? What is needed to get them back on track, and how can their unfulfilled promise be realized?

Chapter 4 explores the forms of analytic and research support required to sustain a fully versatile version of problem-oriented policing, and makes the case that problem-oriented policing is unlikely to reach maturity unless police develop a clearer vision of the analytic support they should be seeking, and analysts and researchers are poised to deliver it. This chapter examines the forms of support traditionally provided to the policing profession by the academic disciplines of criminology and social science, and argues that the nature of research support provided thus far, while valuable, leaves much to be desired. This chapter shows that the current criminological research agenda—focused heavily on program evaluation and "evidence-based policing"—is not only insufficient, but may on occasion stand in the way of operational problem solving.

Chapter 5 looks more carefully at one of the inevitable realities of twenty-first-century policing: the requirement for public police to cooperate effectively with the ubiquitous and ever-growing private-police and security industry. In the United States public safety is provided through a complex patchwork of small organizations—some public, some private, many specialized—as well as through major city, state, and federal law enforcement agencies. The extraordinary growth of private and auxiliary security provision raises obvious public concerns about training standards, levels of professionalism, varieties of motivations, and public accountability.

It was a University of Cincinnati police officer—Ray Tensing—who shot dead an unarmed black motorist, Samuel Dubose, in Cincinnati on July 19, 2015. Officer Tensing had pulled Dubose over for failure to display a front license plate. After some conversation, Dubose attempted to drive away. Tensing claimed that he was being dragged along by Dubose's vehicle and had to shoot.[27] Video evidence from the officer's body camera seemed to contradict that account, and Officer Tensing was subsequently indicted for murder. In announcing the indictment, Hamilton County prosecutor Joe Deters described the incident as "a senseless, asinine shooting."

This event adds one more to the tally of unarmed black men shot dead by white officers. It also adds one more to the much smaller tally of occasions where video evidence undermines an officer's initial justification for a shooting and an indictment for murder follows. But it also raises many questions about the role and powers of campus police, especially as the incident occurred in a public street about one mile away from the campus and the driver involved had no connection to the university. In fact, the University of Cincinnati Police Department, which has seventy-two sworn officers, is a fully accredited police department and its officers have full police powers and receive the standard level of training set out by the Ohio Peace Officer Training Commission (which sets standards for police training across the state of Ohio).[28] Nevertheless, public concerns remain about the various ways in which small departments focused closely on the interests of particular communities (in this instance a university) might differ in their motivation and level of experience from regular public police departments and what manner of controls over their conduct might be needed to protect broader public interests.

Chapter 5 addresses these issues in detail. It stresses the inevitability and benefits of collaboration, but urges caution and the exercise of careful judgment when private motivations and narrower agendas impinge on the provision of public safety.

Chapter 6 makes the case that the law enforcement profession, which has historically tended to be quite isolated, has a great deal in common with a much broader range of governmental organizations (particularly social regulators). All security and social regulatory agencies—including the Coast Guard, environmental protection, customs, immigration, tax, occupational safety and health, and many others—are likewise concerned with controlling risks, reducing harm, and solving problems; and they all use the coercive power of the state to achieve their public purposes. All such agencies have to grapple with common issues: controlling abuses of regulatory power, managing discretion, expanding and managing their compliance tool kit, controlling harmful behaviors and promoting desirable ones, learning the art of problem solving, defining the nature of analytic support, and understanding the role of enforcement in the context of harm reduction (rather than purely investigative) operations. All such agencies have their own analogues for community-oriented and problem-oriented strategies, even though they use different vocabulary to describe these ideas. This chapter makes the case that the police profession could learn much from this broader community and could advance its own strategic development by joining in the wider conversations about regulatory practice and effective risk control.

By focusing on these matters, this volume addresses those aspects of police reform that are truly international in nature and affect the continuing development of policing worldwide. The most obvious audience for this book, therefore, includes anyone and everyone who is concerned about the quality of policing in a democracy. Clearly this includes the police profession itself, but extends far beyond it.

I very much hope the issues raised here will attract a different and broader audience, as well. Chapter 6 makes the case that the police profession has much in common with a broad range of other government agencies, and could learn a great deal by recognizing that and joining in the broader debates about risk-control and harm reduction techniques. But this learning can go both ways. All public agencies with risk-control responsibilities, especially those that use the coercive power of the state in delivering protection, confront all the issues addressed here. They all have to grapple with performance measurement in the context of risk control, and will have little difficulty translating the lessons of chapter 2 into their own setting. Chapter 3 will provide them with an opportunity to consider their own organization's maturity when it comes to constructive engagement with regulated communities, and with the challenges of institutionalizing a mature risk-based (or problem-oriented) approach. All agencies in the risk-control business need to think through the nature of analytic and research support they need, and the benefits and perils of cooperative engagement with multiple parties and across different sectors. Chapters 4 and 5, therefore, raise issues central to regulatory practice and public management more generally.

This book does not delve deeply into those problems that are specifically or especially American. Not because these are unimportant; indeed, they are profoundly important. More because so many others are already paying an enormous amount of attention to these particular issues. I am quite interested in broadening the review of policing theory and strategy in a way that will allow the rest of the policing and regulatory world to learn from America's current crisis without being able to write it all off as a distinctively American set of problems.

For sure, the current spate of high-profile incidents reflects two critical issues that are especially American. First, the persistent and pervasive issues of race in American society, given the long and painful history of racial conflict and struggles over civil rights. Second, the extraordinary levels of police violence, which put American police "off the charts" when compared with their

First World counterparts.[29] These two American issues intersect when police violence appears concentrated on minority groups.

Several of the papers in the recent New Perspectives in Policing series tackle issues of race directly. In "Race and Policing: An Agenda for Action," David Bayley, Michael Davis, and Ronald Davis (currently head of the Community Oriented Policing Office at the Department of Justice) observe that race remains an "American dilemma," especially for police, and they lay out a very broad agenda:

> American police confront issues of race, daily, in almost everything they do. They confront race in the geographic distribution of criminality and the fear of crime as well as in assumptions about what criminals look like. They confront race in the suspicion and hostility of many young African American men they encounter on the street. They confront race in complaints from ethnic communities about being either over- or under-policed. They confront race in charges of racial profiling and unequal justice. And they confront race in decisions about hiring, promoting, and assigning police officers.[30]

Another paper in the series, authored by Anthony Braga and Rod Brunson, examines the issue of black-on-black violence, exploring the statistical and demographic realities of the issue, the common misperceptions, the need for more careful disaggregation and analysis, the dangers of over- or under-policing in minority neighborhoods, and the damaging effect of political ideologies on a genuine search for remedies.[31]

With respect to levels of police violence, other advanced democracies also have their problems. But the levels of police violence in the United States, and sometimes the nature of it, seem both remarkable and appalling.

According to the monitoring now being conducted by the

Washington Post, police in America are currently shooting people dead at an average rate of just under three per day. In the United Kingdom, by contrast, in the five-year period 2010 through 2014, police killed a total of four people, for an average of just less than one *per year*.[32] In the United Kingdom, of course, guns are not so freely available to the public and police are not routinely armed (except in Northern Ireland), so perhaps that is a misleading comparison. Canadian police, who do carry firearms routinely, killed an average of ten people per year in the same five-year period (2010–14).[33] As the *Guardian* newspaper notes, based on its own efforts to collate and catalogue police killings in the United States and elsewhere, on this count, "America is not an outlier . . . it is *the* outlier."[34] German police killed six people in 2011 and seven in 2012. Australian police shot dead ninety-four people in a nineteen-year period (1992–2011). According to the *Guardian*'s tally, U.S. police shot dead ninety-seven people in just one month, March 2015.

America is also an outlier in terms of its liberal gun laws and in permitting open and concealed carrying of weapons. The U.S. homicide rate, also, is *the* outlier when compared with other First World countries. But even when the figures for deaths at the hands of police are corrected for population and for crime rates, American policing stands alone as uniquely lethal. Particularly distressing is the rate at which American police kill unarmed civilians, who, according to the *Guardian*'s 2015 statistics to date, represent roughly 22 percent of those killed by police.[35]

Police violence is not limited, of course, to shootings. Videotaped beatings are surfacing with increasing regularity. Beatings can involve multiple officers standing over a suspect—who is already on the ground and handcuffed or otherwise restrained, no longer posing a physical threat—and punching and kicking them, hitting them with batons, radios, or guns, and for what seems a painfully long time, even for the viewers. We can all be viewers now, thanks to YouTube and the frequency with which such incidents are video-recorded by bystanders or captured on police dash cams or by news helicopters hovering overhead. Videotaped beatings are especially distressing to watch because they make police appear brutal and cruel, and multiple officers appear to be acting that way in concert. In the United States a suspect "taking a beating" is perfectly ordinary police language. This infuriates the public and seems completely baffling to foreigners. Why should anyone ever "take a beating" from police in a modern civilization? Punishment is supposed to be handed out by the criminal justice system, not on the street. The very notion of "delivering a beating" is irreconcilable with the mandate to use minimum necessary force to effect an arrest.

So why does it happen? Many of the most publicized incidents occur at the end of a chase.[36] It doesn't seem to matter much whether the chase was motorized or on foot.

In one recent (April 9, 2015) and extraordinary case, San Bernardino County deputies beat a man, thirty-year-old Francis Jared Pusok, who fled into the Arizona desert, first by car and then on a stolen horse, when the deputies attempted to serve a warrant on him. Eventually, after a chase through the Deep Creek area of Apple Valley that involved more than a dozen officers, several police vehicles, and a police helicopter, the suspect fell off his horse, and appeared in the video to be Tased by one officer. What happened next was captured by a KNBC news helicopter hovering overhead. Pusok lay face down on the ground with his arms outstretched, as if in a posture of surrender. He was eventually surrounded by eleven deputies, who presumably thought it was a police helicopter overhead as they beat the man for about two minutes. According to KNBC's analysis of the videotape, they kicked him seventeen times, punched him thirty-seven times, and struck him with batons four times. Thirteen of the blows were to the head. When the beating was done, Pusok lay motionless on the ground for forty-five minutes, during which time the deputies stood around but provided no medical attention.[37]

To deliver a beating, or a "rough ride," or some other form of physical punishment after a chase seems to be standard practice for some American police departments. The official responses, if and when such videotaped beatings become public, seem mealy-mouthed and inadequate, poor excuses for patently criminal conduct. "The officers were in a state of excitement." "Their judgment was clouded by a rush of adrenalin." "We have to review the circumstances carefully to understand the fuller context." And remedies proposed include "clarifying policy" or "providing supplemental training." But members of the public see the videos, and they know exactly what they see: American police, with alarming frequency, apparently acting with savage cruelty.

Of course we don't know which is increasing: the underlying rate of police beatings or the rate of discovery and exposure to the public through video. Many in the police profession express their hope and belief that discipline is much improved compared with, say, fifty years ago. But the public perception, particularly in minority communities, is that these things have no place at all in American policing and yet they still happen with alarming frequency.

Some of the behaviors captured on video seem baffling. Why do officers behave that way? Are they evil men and women? Did they expect to behave that way when they joined up? Probably not, for the most part. More likely, they have been socialized into a set of beliefs—the subculture of policing—that tolerates, protects, and even promotes such practices.

David Couper was police chief in Madison, Wisconsin, for over twenty years and was much admired for his work in reforming that department. He resigned in 1993 to become an Episcopal priest and has since written three books about policing. He remains extremely active in advocating for a more civilized, humane, and accountable police profession. Major portions of his third book, *Arrested Development*, are autobiographical, and he writes frankly about the way things work within the profession. Based on his long experience, he describes the practice of using extra force when a suspect resists an arrest, runs from police, or fights with them:

> Many departments have problems with officers using excessive force in these situations to punish offenders. When this is a department-wide problem and not just one particular officer's, it will usually be found that it is an accepted practice among the rank and file, and that officers *expect* their colleagues to use extra force in such situations. Of course, many departments look the other way when bad behavior happens, simply calling it understandable in a particular situation.[38]

In a footnote, Couper adds:

> For a good illustration, go to YouTube on the Internet and search "police brutality." Within seconds, you'll see a huge number of videos showing officers after a high-speed chase running up to the vehicle they've pursued and pummeling the driver. This wasn't what they were taught to do and, no doubt, department rules prohibit such behavior—yet it happens because it's simply what many police, as a subculture, do when a chase ends, or even when a person verbally abuses police. In all but the finest police departments there will be some kind of summary beating for those who disregard police authority—that is [those whom police refer to as] "assholes."[39]

According to the *Washington Post* study of 2015 fatal police shootings, dozens of people died while fleeing from police.

"Running is such a provocative act that police experts say there is a name for the injury officers inflict on suspects afterward: a 'foot tax.'"[40]

Others refer to "the code." On July 12, 2000, Thomas Jones and two other suspects were beaten by Philadelphia police after a prolonged car chase. The beating was videotaped and subsequently became public. Fourteen officers were disciplined, but no criminal charges were laid against them.

Nine days after the incident, Christopher Cooper, a former Marine, a former Washington, D.C., metropolitan police officer, and, then, a lawyer, professor of criminal justice, and member of the board of directors of the National Black Police Association, wrote an op-ed piece for the *Philadelphia Inquirer*, which should be essential reading for anyone seeking to understand why beatings occur and why black men are so often the ones beaten. Cooper explains "the code":

> For many Americans not of color, what happened to Thomas Jones is an aberration. For people of color, in particular black people and Latinos, Jones' beating is commonplace police behavior. Another group that knows it's commonplace is police officers themselves.
>
> Sadly, in our early tenure as cops, we are instructed on the "code" of the police subculture. These are norms that are almost always perverse. Two such norms were operable in the Jones mob attack. The first is that if a citizen runs from one of us, we are to beat him severely.
>
> Another is that if a citizen physically hurts one of us, we are to hurt that citizen even more before we bring him to the station. And if that citizen has killed a cop, he shouldn't make it to the station alive. This is well-documented in research literature about policing . . . and in public testimony by police officers.[41]

Cooper's article also stresses the importance of understanding the fundamental dynamics and culture operating within police organizations, rather than focusing on what is provable or not provable in terms of the facts relating to specific incidents of violence:

> Prosecutors fail to realize that the police subculture provides justification for Jones-type beatings long before the beatings ever occur. It teaches police officers how to have a ready excuse to explain away bad behavior. Meanwhile, lay people—DAs, judges, and juries—are willing to accept authoritative versions of what happened on a police scene without question. Such automatic deference, coupled with lay ignorance of the police code, allows police brutality and racially discriminatory policing to flourish.[42]

Christopher Cooper refers to officers who object to such practices or seek to intervene as "code violators," but notes that "all too often, individual officers lack the courage to stand up to that code."

Charles Ramsey, commissioner of police in Philadelphia and cochair of President Obama's Independent Task Force on 21st Century Policing, in his own Perspectives series paper, "The Challenge of Policing in a Democratic Society," also talks about the need for officers to stand up against a subculture that still all too often condones violence and brutality. Ramsey recognizes the courage it takes:

> What about the other officers, the bystanders, when a suspect takes a beating? What is running through those officers' heads? I would guess that there are some with a perverted sense of justice who think everything is fine and that this person deserves this treatment, and I suspect a considerable

number know it is not fine and they are deeply uncomfortable. But what will they do? Will they have the courage to intervene, to step forward, to challenge their colleagues, to do the right thing? Feeling uncomfortable will never be enough. This is a call to action.[43]

Even David Couper admits that as a patrol officer he would not have turned in his police partner:

I . . . realized I was closer to the man I was paired with at work—my partner—than I was to the woman to whom I was married. I shared more of my thoughts, feelings, hopes, and dreams with him than I did with her. Each day at work, I trusted my partner with my life. And then I realized that if he did something wrong, I would no more give him up than I would my own mother.

This is the power of a subculture. . . . I had become a fully-fledged member of what sociologists call [a] subculture; a distinct group of people who have patterns of behavior and beliefs that set them apart from society as a whole.[44]

Ramsey also notes that progress in rooting out such practices will remain slow unless profound changes occur in the ways whistleblowers or code violators are treated:

Our systems and organizational cultures often fail to support or reward that kind of courage. When an officer reports misconduct to internal affairs, what kind of reward does he or she get for such courage? Too often, it seems as if the incentives and reward structures are stacked against those who are on the side of right. Too often, those who speak up or say "no" end up ostracized and decide never to do that again— because of the way the department treats them, because of the cost that the system imposes on them. At some point that has got to change if we expect reality to be different in ten or twenty years.[45]

We must surely expect reality to be different in ten or twenty years. Hopefully the current crisis in American policing and continued public and judicial scrutiny of policing practices will mean we do not have to wait that long.

To move reforms along, though, it surely helps to be clear what that different reality should be. As the federal inquiry into the Ferguson Police Department shows, once you look past the specific incidents and search out the underlying forces and dynamics at work, one ends up hankering for something akin to a genuine and mature implementation of community and problem-oriented policing.

This book focuses deliberately on those issues that, while they may be reflected in the current American crisis, are not uniquely American. It is worth noting that these aspirations about the nature and quality of policing are by no means just American, either. Citizens of any mature democracy can expect and should demand police services that are responsive to their needs, tolerant of diversity, and skillful in unraveling and tackling crime and other community problems. They should expect and demand that police officers are decent, courteous, humane, sparing and skillful in the use of force, respectful of citizens' rights, disciplined, and professional. These are ordinary, reasonable expectations.

But whenever someone advocates for community policing, others object, pointing to the lack of convincing evidence in the research literature that community policing is effective in controlling crime. There are some rather clear reasons for that lack of evidence, including the fact that community policing in many departments has been mere rhetoric, and, even where community policing has been implemented in ways that affect operations, the variations in form between departments are too great to permit reliable evaluation.[46]

But more fundamentally, it seems that researchers ask the wrong question. If one regards crime control as the "bottom line of policing," then one might assess policing styles and strategies solely in terms of how much they contribute to the singular purpose of reducing reported crime.

Community policing is not merely a device for controlling crime. Rather, effective crime control is just one component of community policing. Community policing is an end in itself. It is an entitlement. From a public perspective it is vital to work out, finally, how this model of policing can be delivered in a mature and sustainable way. The current crisis in American policing makes that much, at least, quite clear.

TWO

Defining Success

Perhaps everything the modern police executive needs to know about defining the mission, setting goals, and measuring performance has already been written. But much of the best work on the subject is both voluminous and more than a decade old, so there is no guarantee that today's police executives have read it. Indeed, it appears that many police organizations have not yet taken some of the most important lessons to heart.

The Ferguson Police Department apparently settled on a totally inappropriate mission, raising revenue, and then organized virtually every aspect of its operations around that distorted sense of purpose. The New York Police Department (NYPD) has for many years focused closely on reducing crime numbers as the "bottom line" of policing. So have many other police departments, especially those that have copied the NYPD's CompStat system and used it as a managerial system to drive the crime-reduction imperative. These departments may not have understood the dangers that arise when an organization places intense pressure on its staff to produce one single and particular outcome without imposing adequate controls on the methods they might use. Society pays a price when other dimensions of performance get relatively short shrift.

In this chapter I hope to offer some broad frameworks for recognizing the value of police work, to point out common mistakes regarding performance measurement, and to draw police executives' attention to key pieces of literature that they might not have explored and may find useful. I also hope to bring to the police profession some of the general lessons learned in other security and regulatory professions about the special challenges of performance measurement in a risk-control or harm-reduction setting.

A research project titled "Measuring What Matters," funded jointly by the National Institute of Justice (NIJ) and the Office of Community Oriented Policing Services (COPS), led to the publication in July 1999 of a substantial collection of essays on the subject of measuring performance.[1] The fifteen essays that make up that collection are fascinating, not least for the divergence of opinion they reveal among the experts of the day. The sharpest disagreements pit the champions of the NYPD's early CompStat model (with its rigorous and almost single-minded focus on reductions in reported crime) against a broad range of scholars who mostly espoused more expansive conceptions of the policing mission and pressed the case for more inclusive and more nuanced approaches to performance measurement.

Three years later, in 2002, the Police Executive Research Forum (PERF) published another major report on performance measurement, *Recognizing Value in Policing: The Challenge of Recognizing Police Performance,* authored principally by Mark H. Moore.[2] PERF followed that up in 2003 with a condensed document, *The "Bottom Line" of Policing: What Citizens Should Value (and Measure!) in Police Performance,*[3] authored by Moore and Anthony Braga.

Despite the richness of the frameworks presented in these

and other materials, a significant proportion of today's police organizations remain narrowly focused on the same categories of indicators that have dominated the field for decades:

1. Reductions in the number of serious crimes reported, most commonly presented as local comparisons against an immediately preceding time period
2. Clearance rates
3. Response times
4. Measures of enforcement productivity (for example, numbers of arrests, citations, or stop-and-frisk searches)

A few departments now use citizen satisfaction surveys on a regular basis, but most do not. Clearance rates are generally difficult to measure in a standardized and objective fashion, so category 2, clearance rates, tends to receive less emphasis than the other three. Categories 3 and 4—response times and enforcement productivity metrics—are useful in showing that police are getting to calls fast and working hard but reveal nothing about whether they are working intelligently, using appropriate methods, or having a positive impact.

Therefore, category 1—reductions in the number of serious crime reports—tends to dominate many departments' internal and external claims of success, being the closest thing available to a genuine crime-control outcome measure.

There is much to be said, of course, for focusing an organization's attention on things that matter. It prevents an organization from spinning its wheels, scattering its efforts, or continuing in a variety of practices that have little or no measurable effect. But focusing on too narrow a set of measures can result in an organization neglecting other important dimensions of performance and relying on metrics without understanding the potentially misleading effects of taking them out of context.

The four standard sets of measures listed above have retained their prominence despite everything the field is supposed to have learned in the last twenty years about the limitations of reported crime statistics. Those limitations, to be explored later, include the following:

- The focus is narrow, because crime control is just one of several components of the police mission.
- The focus on serious crimes is narrower still, as community concerns often revolve around other problems and patterns of behavior.
- Relentless pressure to lower the numbers, without equivalent pressure to preserve the integrity of the recording and reporting systems, invites manipulation of crime statistics (suppression of reports and misclassification of crimes) and other forms of corruption.
- Focusing on reported crime overlooks unreported crimes. Overall levels of victimization are generally two to three times higher than reported crime rates.[4] Particularly low reporting rates apply to household thefts, rape, other sexual assaults, crimes against youths aged twelve to seventeen, violent crimes committed at schools, and crimes committed by someone the victim knows well.[5]
- Pressure to reduce the numbers is counterproductive when dealing with invisible crimes (classically unreported or underreported crimes, such as crimes within the family, white-collar crimes, consensual crimes such as drug dealing or bribery, and crimes involving intimidation). Successful campaigns against these types of crime often involve deliberate attempts to expose the problem by first driving reporting rates up, not down.[6]
- A focus on crime rate reductions does not consider the costs or side effects of the strategies used to achieve them.

- Emphasizing comparisons with prior time periods affords a short-term and very local perspective. It may give a department the chance to boast even while its crime rates remain abysmal compared with other jurisdictions. Conversely, best performers (with low crime rates overall) might look bad when random fluctuations on a quarterly or annual basis raise their numbers. Genuine, longer-term trends may be masked by temporary changes, such as those caused by weather patterns or special events. More important than local short-term fluctuations are sustained longer-term trends and comparisons with crime rates in similar communities. Pressure to beat one's own performance year after year can produce bizarre and perverse incentives.
- Even if crime levels were once out of control, the reductions achievable will inevitably run out when rates plateau at more acceptable levels. At this point, the department's normal crime-control success story—assuming that reductions in reported crime rates had been its heart and soul—evaporates. Some executives fail to recognize the point at which legitimate reductions have been exhausted. Continuing to demand reductions at that point is like failing to set the torque control on a power screwdriver. First you drive the screw, which is useful work; but then you rip everything to shreds and even undo the value of your initial tightening. The same performance focus that initially produced legitimate gains becomes a destructive force if pressed too hard or for too long.
- A number is just a number, and reliance only on numbers reduces all the complexity of real life to a zero or a one. One special crime, or one particular crime unsolved, may have a disproportionate impact on a community's sense of safety and security. Aggregate numbers fail to capture the significance of special cases.

Reported crime rates will always belong among the suite of indicators relevant for managing a complex police department, as will response times, clearance rates, enforcement productivity, community satisfaction, and indicators of morale. But what will happen if police executives stress one or another of these to the virtual exclusion of all else? What if they fail to monitor or adequately control the choice of methods, the use of force, the effect on communities, or the integrity of the recording and reporting systems? From the public's perspective, the resulting organizational behaviors can be disastrous.

If we acknowledged the limitations of reported crime rates and managed to lessen our dependence on them, then how would we recognize true success in crime control? And how might we better capture and describe it?

I believe the answer is the same across the full range of government's risk-control responsibilities, whether the harms to be controlled are criminal victimization, pollution, corruption, fraud, tax evasion, terrorism, or other potential and actual harms. The definition of success in risk control or harm reduction is to spot emerging problems early and then suppress them before they do much harm.[7] This is a very different idea from "allow problems to grow so hopelessly out of control that we can then get serious, all of a sudden, and produce substantial reductions year after year after year."

What do citizens expect of government agencies entrusted with crime control, risk control, or other harm reduction duties? The public does not expect that governments will be able to prevent all crimes or contain all harms. But they do expect government agencies to provide the best protection possible, and at a reasonable price, by being:

- Vigilant, so they can spot emerging threats early, pick up on precursors and warning signs, use their imaginations to work out what could happen, use their intelligence systems to discover what others are planning, and do all this before much harm is done.

- Nimble, flexible enough to organize themselves quickly and appropriately around each emerging crime pattern rather than being locked into routines and processes designed for traditional issues.
- Skillful, masters of the entire intervention tool kit, experienced (as craftsmen) in picking the best tools for each task, and adept at inventing new approaches when existing methods turn out to be irrelevant or insufficient to suppress an emerging threat.[8]

Real success in crime control—spotting emerging crime problems early and suppressing them before they do much harm—would not produce substantial year-to-year reductions in crime figures, because genuine and substantial reductions are available only when crime problems have first grown out of control. Neither would best practices produce enormous numbers of arrests, coercive interventions, or any other specific activity, because skill demands economy in the use of force and financial resources and rests on artful and well-tailored responses rather than extensive and costly campaigns. Ironically, therefore, the two classes of metrics that still seem to wield the most influence in many departments—crime reduction and enforcement productivity—would utterly fail to reflect the very best performance in crime control.

Further, we must take seriously the fact that other important duties of the police will never be captured through crime statistics or in measures of enforcement output. As NYPD Assistant Commissioner Ronald J. Wilhelmy wrote in a November 2013 internal NYPD strategy document:

We cannot continue to evaluate personnel on the simple measure of whether crime is up or down relative to a prior period. Most importantly, CompStat has ignored measurement of other core functions. Chiefly, we fail to measure what may be our highest priority: public satisfaction. We also fail to measure quality of life, integrity, community relations, administrative efficiency, and employee satisfaction, to name just a few other important areas.[9]

Who Is Flying This Airplane, and What Kind of Training Have They Had?

Photograph by Christiaan Van Heijst, www.jpcvanheijst.com, used with permission.

At one recent meeting of the Executive Session on Policing and Public Safety, we asked the police chiefs present, "Do you think your police department is more or less complicated than a Boeing 737?" (See photograph of Boeing 737 cockpit.) They all concluded fairly quickly that they considered their departments more complicated and put forward various reasons for that opinion.

First, their departments were made up mostly of people, whom they regarded as more complex and difficult to manage than the electrical, mechanical, hydraulic, and software systems that make up a modern commercial jetliner. Second, they felt their departments' missions were multiple and ambiguous rather than single and clear.

Picking Denver as a prototypical flight destination, they wondered aloud, "What's the equivalent of Denver for my police department?" Given a destination, flight paths can be mapped out in advance and scheduled within a minute, even across the globe. Unless something strange or unusual happens along the way, the airline pilot (and most likely an autopilot) follows the plan. For police agencies, "strange and unusual" is normal. Unexpected events happen all the time, often shifting a department's priorities and course. As a routine matter, different constituencies have different priorities, obliging police executives to juggle conflicting and sometimes irreconcilable demands.

Assuming that for these or other reasons, the answer is "more complicated," then we might want to know how the training and practices of police executives compare with those of commercial pilots when it comes to using information in managing their enterprise.

The pilot of a Boeing 737 has access to at least fifty types of information on a continuing basis. Not all of them require constant monitoring, as some of the instruments in the cockpit beep or squeak or flash when they need attention. At least ten to twelve types of information are monitored constantly. What do we expect of pilots? That they know, through their training, how to combine different types of information and interpret them in context so they can quickly recognize important conditions of the plane and of the environment and know how they should respond.

A simple question like "Am I in danger of stalling?" (that is, flying too slowly to retain control of the aircraft) requires at least seven types of information to resolve—altitude, air temperature, wind speed, engine power, flap deployment, weight, and weight distribution—together with knowledge of the technical parameters that determine the edge of the flight envelope. Some of these factors relate to the plane and some relate to external conditions. All these indicators must be combined to identify a potential stall.

Thanks to the availability of simulators, commercial airline pilots are now trained to recognize and deal with an amazing array of possible scenarios, many of which they will never encounter in real life.[10] They learn how various scenarios would manifest themselves through a variety of indicators so they can recognize them quickly, diagnose them accurately, and respond appropriately.

With so many forms of information available to the pilot, we might wonder how many of the dials in the cockpit are designated key performance indicators or, for that matter, how many of them are regarded as performance indicators at all. The answer is none. No single dial in the cockpit tells the pilot how well he or she is doing, or is used to judge performance. Airline pilots appreciate and use an extensive array of different types of information—habitually use them in combination and in relation to one another—but are very slow to label any of them performance indicators.

By contrast, many public sector agencies (this problem is by no means confined to police departments) pay close attention to a comparatively small number of indicators and seem all too keen to select one or two of them (usually no more than five) as key performance indicators. Designating a measure as a performance indicator usually means we determine in advance whether we expect it to move up or down, and we may even set a particular level as a target. Public sector executives then often seem surprised when the narrow range of information monitored produces partial or inadequate interpretations of what is really happening and when the narrow performance focus drives behaviors that turn out to be perverse and contrary to the public interest.

Executive Session participants were quick to point out the lack of "simulator training" currently available for senior police managers. Simulations in the form of practical exercises are frequently used in entry-level training for recruits and in training courses for specialty functions (for example, hostage negotiations or SWAT). For executives, simulator-style training is occasionally available in crisis leadership courses, where trainees are invited to take their turn at the helm in a crisis response exercise. But absent a crisis, most executive teams operate without any special training to help them interpret the myriad signals available or recognize important conditions quickly and pick the best response to different scenarios.

In the absence of such training, many executive teams muddle through, having learned most of what they know through their own experience on the way up through the managerial ranks rather than through formal training. As one chief noted, the closest equivalent to executive-level simulator training is when one department has the opportunity to learn from the misery of another. A collegial network of police executives, ready to share both their successes and failures, is a valuable asset to the profession (see box 2-1).

Any numbers game is, of course, a simplification. Carl Klockars expresses this beautifully (and with a nod to Arthur "Dooley" Wilson) in *Measuring What Matters*:

> In every instance of measurement, the conversion of a thing, event, or occasion to a number requires ignoring or discarding all other meaning that thing, event, or occasion might have.

BOX 2-1. Scenarios for Police Executives

Imagining a simulator for police executives might be interesting. Here are three scenarios:

1. You notice the following:
   - The conviction rate for cases prosecuted is unusually low and falling.
   - The proportion of complaints against officers that are internally generated is rising.
   - The number of internal requests for transfers is unusually high, as is the use of sick days.
   - Based on community surveys, public confidence in the agency is rising, but the response rate on surveys is falling.
   - The reported crime rate is dropping fast.

   What is happening? What else would you want to know? What might you do?

2. You notice the following:
   - Drug-related arrests are up 30 percent over last year.
   - The department has just (proudly) announced "record drug seizures" for the last quarter.
   - The proportion of drug-related prosecutions that result in jail terms has fallen to record low levels.
   - Street-level drug prices are at record lows.

   What is happening? What else would you want to know? What might you do?

3. You notice the following:
   - The number of domestic violence calls received by the department has risen sharply over the last six months.
   - The number of homicides determined to be domestic violence related has dropped by one-third in the same period.
   - The proportion of domestic violence arrests that result in charges has just dropped below 40 percent for the first time.

- The proportion of domestic violence cases prosecuted that result in convictions has also fallen below 70 percent for the first time.

What is happening? What else would you want to know? What might you do?

These three scenarios were presented to the Executive Session in the context of our discussions on performance measurement. Given the time limitations, we did not have the chance to explore them at length, and none of the police leaders present ventured an opinion as to what he or she thought might be happening in each case. But they did agree that they would quite likely reach very different conclusions from one another, given their varied experiences and biases.

These scenarios are relatively simple ones, involving only four or five indicators. Even so, using these indicators in combination and treating them as important management information might lead one to very different conclusions than treating one or another of them as a performance metric and specifying whether it should move up or down or reach some target level.

Scenario 1 might reveal an agency in crisis with plummeting morale. The community may be giving up on the police, no longer bothering to report crimes. Only "friends of the department" bother to respond to surveys; everyone else has given up on them. Corruption problems may be surfacing, evidenced by a higher rate of internally generated complaints and loss of cases in court, perhaps due to tainted evidence or community distrust.

Scenario 2 might suggest a failing drug-control strategy, with numerous arrests exhausting the capacity of the justice system but no positive or structural impact on the drug problem.

Scenario 3 might reveal the early stages of an energetic and successful campaign against domestic violence, which is helping to expose the problem more effectively while using arrests and prosecutions aggressively as deterrence tactics (even if prosecutions are not taken all the way through the system).

Notice that the two scenarios suggesting various forms of failure and trouble (1 and 2) show a reduction in reported crime rates (traditionally regarded as a sign of success). One of them (scenario 2) shows high levels of enforcement productivity.

The only story here that suggests an effective crime-control strategy (scenario 3) shows an increase in reported crime rates and a decrease in the conviction rate (traditionally signals of poor performance).

Even these relatively straightforward examples show how too close a focus on one or two classes of metric could blind an organization to meaning and context and possibly mislead everyone about what is really happening.

The easy way to appreciate this very hard point in all its paradox and irony is to remember this: a kiss is just a kiss, a sigh is just a sigh, and a crime is just a crime, as time goes by. (Which, of course, anyone who has kissed, sighed, or committed, investigated, or been the victim of a crime knows is not true.)[11]

Filmmakers and writers of police television dramas have picked up on the collision that happens, somewhere in the middle ranks of a police department, between high-level general strategies (often numbers driven) and the rich texture of real life. It does not really matter whether one is watching Detective McNulty in *The Wire*, Detective Chief Superintendent Foyle in *Foyle's War*, or any other fictional mid-rank police officer.

At some point in most episodes an assistant commissioner or other senior officer is going to show up unexpectedly at the local police station. Never is his visit good news! The senior officers are invariably portrayed as interfering nitwits, ignorant and dismissive of what is happening at the street level. Often, they appear with their own new pet initiatives, requiring this many cases to be made or that many arrests of a particular type. Their agendas seem motivated by political, personal, or career-enhancing imperatives, or are blatantly corrupt. The senior officers never listen and never help, but walk in with their general solutions that are not well thought out and demand a campaign of arrests or prosecutions that they claim will serve as a visible public demonstration of how seriously the department takes such-and-such an issue. Such visits interrupt valuable work and create imperatives for frontline officers that seem unhelpful, absurd, or not in the public interest. Morale suffers, and the star of the show is left to fend off the ridiculous pressures from above so his or her subordinates can carry on with "real police work," knowing full well it will never be recognized by the department.

Of course, incompetent and corrupt senior management always makes for good theater. But the creators of police dramas do seem to have picked up on a specific organizational dynamic relevant to policing. Each episode is about a specific scenario, which has all the quirky peculiarities of real life. That is what makes each episode unique, interesting, and worth watching. The senior officers are unflatteringly portrayed as besotted with a general strategy and a narrow performance focus, neither of which does justice to the complex and varied nature of police work.

If a department appreciates that complexity, does well on vigilance, nimbleness, and skill, and therefore excels at spotting emerging problems early and suppressing them before they do much harm, what will success look like? How will such a department demonstrate its crime control expertise?

The answer is that evaluation of performance will consist largely of problem-specific project accounts describing emerging crime patterns and what happened to each one. Each project account will describe how the department spotted the problem in the first place, how it analyzed and subsequently understood the problem, what the department and its partners did about the problem, and what happened as a result. Some in policing call that the scanning, analysis, response, and assessment (SARA) model. It is a straightforward problem-oriented account that has little to do with aggregate numbers of any particular kind.

Broader Frameworks for Monitoring and Measurement

If the analogy of the cockpit turns out to be useful, then the following sections may help senior managers develop a broader sense of the banks of instruments they might want to have available in their cockpits and a clearer sense of how to use them for different purposes. To understand the diversity of indicators that could be relevant and useful in a police department's cockpit, we should remember: the breadth of the policing mission; the multiple dimensions of performance that are therefore relevant; the different managerial purposes that measurement can serve; and the different types of work that occur within an agency, each of which naturally generates different types of information.

Much literature is available on all of these subjects, but for the sake of efficiency, I will refer readers to one principal author for each: Herman Goldstein for breadth of mission;[12] Mark Moore for multiple dimensions of performance;[13] Robert Behn for different managerial purposes;[14] and my own work on operational risk control for different types of work.[15]

Broadening the Frame: The Mission of Policing

In his book *Policing a Free Society*, Herman Goldstein summarized the functions of the police:[16]

- Prevent and control conduct widely recognized as threatening to life and property (serious crime).
- Aid individuals who are in danger of physical harm, such as the victims of criminal attacks.
- Protect constitutional guarantees, such as the right of free speech and assembly.
- Facilitate the movement of people and vehicles.
- Assist those who cannot care for themselves: the intoxicated, the addicted, the mentally ill, the physically disabled, the old, and the young.
- Resolve conflict, whether between individuals, groups of individuals, or individuals and their government.
- Identify problems that have the potential to become more serious for the individual citizen, the police, or the government.
- Create and maintain a feeling of security in the community.

This template, now thirty-seven years old, seems a solid place to start and perfectly usable today as a frame for describing the multiple components of the police mission. Each of the eight areas Goldstein mentions might constitute one chapter in a police department's annual report. Perhaps at the outset the first chapter (crime control) might be more thickly populated than some of the others, but with some effort a better balance might be achieved.

Goldstein's framework pushes police to view their role more broadly than as part of the criminal justice system. The community policing movement and the evolution of CompStat systems into broader CitiStat systems have, together, pushed police departments further in recognizing their role as a part of municipal government.[17] As Moore and Poethig point out in an essay in *Measuring What Matters*:

If we conceive of the police as nothing more than "the first step in the criminal justice system," then we might easily miss the contributions that they make "outside the box" of crime control, law enforcement, and arresting people. On the other hand, if we conceive of the police as an agency of municipal government that shares with other agencies the broad responsibility for strengthening the quality of urban life, then we are in a better position to notice that the police contribute much more to those goals than is captured by the simple idea of reducing crime. We also notice that the police have capabilities that go far beyond their ability to make arrests and that these capabilities are valuable to the enterprise of city government. In short, the police are a more valuable asset when viewed from the vantage point of trying to strengthen urban life than they are when viewed from the narrower perspective of reducing crime through making arrests.[18]

An obvious example of this broader role, as Moore and Poethig point out, is emergency response:

Partly because the police department is the only agency that works twenty-four hours a day, seven days a week, and makes house calls, police will continue to be the "first responders" to a wide variety of emergencies. These emergencies can be medical (although ambulance services increasingly take care of these) or they can be social, such as deranged people threatening themselves or others, homeless children found wandering the streets with no parents to care for them, or drunks at risk of freezing to death after falling asleep on a park bench.[19]

The terrorist attacks of September 11, 2001, brought another kind of multi-agency network to the fore. Police departments, especially those in major cities, were now required (and with no diminution of their other responsibilities) to participate in a range of counterterrorism, domestic security, and intelligence collaborations at regional, national, and international levels. Reporting systems that focused too heavily on local crime statistics would likely overlook their contributions on this front. Of course, much of the work conducted in the security domain cannot be discussed in public as readily as routine crime control activities. Nevertheless, it would be a shame not to include this aspect of the modern police mission in a department's performance account, even if parts of the story could only be presented to those stakeholders authorized to hear it.

Broadening the Frame: Dimensions of Performance

Working from Goldstein's (and other commentators') broader sense of the policing mission, Mark Moore develops a framework for holding police departments accountable. In *Recognizing Value in Policing: The Challenge of Measuring Police Performance*, he and his coauthors explore the range of data types and methods of observation that could provide a basis for assessing police performance in each of the following seven dimensions:[20]

- Reducing criminal victimization
- Calling offenders to account
- Reducing fear and enhancing personal security
- Guaranteeing safety in public spaces (including traffic safety)
- Using financial resources fairly, efficiently, and effectively
- Using force and authority fairly, efficiently, and effectively
- Satisfying customer demands/achieving legitimacy with those policed

Moore notes that reported crime statistics only partially capture levels of criminal victimization, and that criminal victimization is only one of the seven dimensions of performance that matter to the public. In particular he takes issue with the notion that crime statistics should be treated as the "bottom line" of policing. William J. Bratton stated this view in an essay he contributed to NIJ's *Measuring What Matters*: "Crime statistics have become the department's bottom line, the best indicator of how the police are doing, precinct by precinct and citywide."[21]

Moore says the analogy with a commercial firm's bottom line is flawed because the crime statistics themselves do not capture the costs of the methods used to achieve them. Reductions in crime levels ought, he says, to be treated as part of gross revenues (not net revenues). The use by police of financial resources and, especially, the use of force or authority should be regarded as costs and, therefore, counted against the revenues.[22] The "bottom line" is, therefore, served if police manage to bring down crime rates and are economical with their uses of force and money. "Crime reduction is closer to the idea of the *gross revenues* a private company earns by producing and selling particular products and services, not its *profit*. . . . Managers ought to be interested in trying to widen the difference between the valuable results the police produce (reduced crime), and the costs incurred in producing those results."[23]

In the early days of CompStat in New York City, with widespread use of aggressive street order maintenance tactics, it did not appear that huge numbers of arrests were regarded as a cost. In fact, the number of arrests seems to have been a source of pride for the department. George Kelling, in the essay he contributed to *Measuring What Matters*, commented: "Even by more widely touted measurements, New York police do relatively well; so many people have been arrested that neither jails nor prisons can hold them. If the number of cells was expanded, few doubt that New York City police could fill almost any added capacity as well."[24]

Carl Klockars, in his essay for *Measuring What Matters*, stressed the importance of the skill of minimizing the use of force. He points out how much officers vary in this regard and in their predisposition to resort to violent or nonviolent means to exercise control in their encounters with civilians: "In any police agency there are officers who are well known for their ability to walk into an out-of-control situation and stabilize it peacefully. (There are others, of course, who can turn any situation into a riot.) The skill of such officers is [in] knowing how to work in ways that minimize the use of force."[25]

Stuart Scheingold, in his essay for *Measuring What Matters*, warned that the "kinds of police practices associated with zero-tolerance and hyper law enforcement seem likely to increase the mistrust of the police that robs crime control of its consensus building capacity."[26] Scheingold also recalls the warnings about the effects of zero tolerance and hyper law enforcement that Wesley Skogan provided in his 1990 book *Disorder and Decline: Crime and the Spiral of Decay in American Neighborhoods*: "Even if they are conducted in a strictly legal fashion, aggressive tactics such as saturating areas with police, stopping cars frequently, conducting extensive field interrogations and searches, and bursting into apartments suspected of harboring gambling or drugs can undermine police-community relations in black and Hispanic neighborhoods."[27]

The underlying tensions between police and predominantly minority communities may amplify these costs, according to Skogan, because "residents of poor and minority neighborhoods with serious disorder problems often have antagonistic relations with the police. They regard the police as another of their problems, frequently perceiving them to be arrogant, brutal, racist, and corrupt."[28]

Moore, along with these and many other commentators, has urged police to recognize coercive power as a precious commodity to be used sparingly and invites them to search for artful interventions that use authority efficiently rather than defaulting to massive enforcement campaigns of one kind or another.[29] The point is not to rule out enforcement campaigns where these are required. Rather, the point is that a full accounting of police performance demands serious attention to the costs as well as to the gross revenues of such campaigns.

Moore also proposes an expansive view of client satisfaction that includes an assessment of the experience of those arrested or cited. Not that we would expect them to be pleased that they were caught! But we would hope to hear that their rights were respected, that excessive force was not used against them, and that they were treated with dignity and courtesy even while being brought to book.[30]

Broadening the Frame: Purposes of Measuring Performance

Robert Behn's 2003 article, "Why Measure Performance? Different Purposes Require Different Measures,"[31] has recently been celebrated as one of the most influential articles in the history of the journal in which it was published, the *Public Administration Review*. I often recommend this as foundational reading for practitioners wanting to rethink their department's use of metrics and indicators.

In this article, Behn lays out eight different managerial purposes that may be served by various types of performance measurement and monitoring. His summary has been reproduced here as table 2-1. Behn explores the different types of indicators that serve these eight managerial purposes.[32] For example, evaluation of agency performance at the aggregate level (purpose 1) involves attempts to link agency outputs with societal outcomes and needs to consider the effects of exogenous factors. Motivating teams internally (purpose 4) may use real-time, functionally specific activity and productivity metrics disaggregated to the team level. These might be compared with production targets or even pitted against one another in an internal competition.

Organizational learning (purpose 7) may rest more on disaggregated data that can reveal anomalies and deviations from norms, revealing problems to be understood and resolved. Improvement of departmental processes (purpose 8) requires linking internal process design changes with their effects on agency outputs, efficiency, and outcomes.

Broadening the Frame: Recognizing Different Types of Work

The fourth way to broaden the frame is to recognize the characteristics of different classes of work that coexist within a complex organization.

First, and most familiar, is functional work, which groups workers with other similarly skilled workers. Investigators work together within a detective bureau, auditors in the audit bureau, educators in the training department, and lawyers in the general counsel's office. Functional professionalism requires staying current, skilled, and state-of-the-art.

For any specialist functional unit, the most readily available metrics cover quantity and quality. Quantity is easiest to measure: how many cases opened and closed, how many audits com-

TABLE 2-1. Eight Purposes Available to Public Managers for Measuring Performance

Purpose	Public manager's question that the performance measure can help answer
1 **Evaluate**	How well is my public agency performing?
2 **Control**	How can I ensure that my subordinates are doing the right thing?
3 **Budget**	On what programs, people, or projects should my agency spend the public's money?
4 **Motivate**	How can I motivate line staff, middle managers, nonprofit and for-profit collaborators, stakeholders, and citizens to do the things necessary to improve performance?
5 **Promote**	How can I convince political superiors, legislators, stakeholders, journalists, and citizens that my agency is doing a good job?
6 **Celebrate**	What accomplishments are worthy of the important organizational ritual of celebrating success?
7 **Learn**	Why is what working or not working?
8 **Improve**	What exactly should who do differently to improve performance?

Source: Table 1 in Robert D. Behn, "Why Measure Performance? Different Purposes Require Different Measures," *Public Administration Review* 63, no.5 (September/October 2003), pp. 586–606.

pleted, how many hours of training delivered. But each function should also have and emphasize its own quality metrics lest concerns over quantity drown out concerns over quality. Ideas about quality may include indications of significance or relevance (of a case or an audit) as well as assessments of whether the activities are conducted more or less professionally. A functional unit, if it divides its output quantity by its inputs, may also furnish indications of productivity or efficiency (for example, the number of cases closed per investigator, the number of audits completed per auditor, or the number of training hours delivered per instructor).

Second, and also familiar, is process-based work. By this I mean any kind of transactional work that is repeated hundreds or thousands of times. Obvious examples include tax agencies processing tax returns, environmental agencies issuing or renewing environmental permits for industry, a licensing authority processing applications, as well as police departments responding to emergency calls or to complaints from the public about officer conduct. Given the repetitive nature and volume of such work, organizations invest in process design (involving procedures, protocols, automation, and flow patterns) to handle the loads in expeditious, smooth, and predictable ways.

Five categories of management information are associated with every process:

- Volume: measures of transaction volume (and trends in volume over time). This is important management information, as it affects resource allocation decisions, even though the incoming volume may not be under the organization's control.
- Timeliness: how long it takes to process transactions. Many processes have mandatory timelines. Measures used may include average processing times, worst-case times, or

percentage of the transaction load that is handled within mandated or specified time periods.

- Accuracy: the proportion of the determinations or judgments made that turn out to be "correct." Metrics on accuracy usually come from case reviews or audits of samples conducted after the fact. Getting a decision right early is preferable to getting it right eventually (after review or on appeal), as it is quicker, cheaper, and generally more satisfactory for all the stakeholders.
- Cost efficiency: indicators of the cost of running the process divided by the transaction volume. Processing costs per transaction can be driven down through process improvement, process redesign, and automation.
- Client satisfaction: Almost every process transaction involves a client (a caller, a complainant, an applicant). Clients can be sampled and surveyed retrospectively to determine the nature of their experience with the process. Even if the client did not get the decision he or she wanted, he or she can still legitimately comment on whether the process seemed fair and efficient and whether he or she was treated properly.

The third type of work—risk-based work—differs from functional work and process work. In the vocabulary of the police profession, the most familiar phrase for this would be problem-oriented work. It is not about one particular method (functional), and it is not about quality management in the context of an established process; rather, it is about a specific risk concentration, issue, or problem. For risk-based work, professionalism begins with spotting problems early and discerning their character and dynamics long before anyone decides which tactics might be relevant or whether any of the organization's routine processes touch the problem at all.

This extract from *The Character of Harms* describes some

of the frustrations that arise when agencies depend too heavily on functional and process-based metrics and fail to recognize problem-oriented or risk-based work as different:

> Even the combination of [the functional and process-based] performance stories falls short with respect to demonstrating effective harm-control. It might show the agency worked hard to apply the functional tools it has, and that it operated its established processes with alacrity and precision. But it leaves open the question of whether tool selection is effective, and whether the processes established touch the pressing issues of the day. The audience can see agencies working hard, which they like. But they would like to be convinced they are also working effectively on the problems they choose to address, and that they are identifying and selecting the most important issues to address. Neither the function-based performance story (for example, "we completed this many high-quality investigations") nor the process-based version ("we cleared our backlogs and streamlined our system") provide such assurance.[33]

The risk-based or problem-oriented performance story is quite different from the other two. It consists of a collection of project-based accounts, each comprising five elements:[34]

1. A description of the data or intelligence that alerted the department to the problem and showed it to be of sufficient scope and significance to warrant special attention
2. A description of the metrics selected (which are project-specific) to be used in determining whether the condition "got better"; in other words, outcome or impact metrics through which project success or failure might be judged
3. A description of the action plan adopted and maybe a second or third one used if and when it was determined that the first one failed

4. A description of what happened to the project metrics over time and how the project team interpreted those changes

5. A decision about project closure, hopefully with the problem sufficiently abated that resources could be withdrawn so the department could move on to the next pressing issue. Continuing attention to the problem would enter a longer-term (and less resource-intensive) monitoring and maintenance phase.

If a department succeeds in its crime-control mission, the heart of its success story will be the collection of project-based accounts, each describing an emerging crime pattern spotted early and dealt with skillfully. The more vigilant the department becomes in spotting emerging problems early, the less available significant crime reductions will be. Aggregate levels of crime may remain low but relatively steady, even as the department works hard to spot new threats before they have a chance to grow out of control.

Criminologists and other evaluators of police performance—who tend to use changes in the aggregate reported crime rate as the outcome variable in their analysis—may not recognize best practice, as the crime reductions visible at the aggregate level may not be statistically significant or may not be present at all.[35]

However, the risk-based performance account—which describes how the department kept the aggregate rates low—is always available. That account relies much less on aggregate crime numbers and, instead, describes the collection of problem-specific interventions. Relevant metrics are tailored to each project and derive from disaggregated data filtered to fit the problem being addressed.

Setting Goals Using Performance Metrics

With the distinctions between functional, process-based, and risk-based work clarified, it might be worth observing which types of metrics associated with each type of work could or should be used for goal setting—that is, as performance metrics.

Some departments set targets for functional outputs, including enforcement activities such as arrests, stops, searches, and traffic citations. This only makes sense in particular circumstances and should never be the default position or become normal practice. If you want quality work from a carpenter, it makes no sense to demand that he or she drill a certain number of holes or hammer a quota of nails. The essence of craftsmanship involves mastery of all the tools and the ability to select among them based on a clear understanding of the specific task in hand. Functional quotas make little sense in this context.

The use of quotas for enforcement activity is always contentious, subject to officer whistleblowing and media scrutiny.[36] The danger is that setting enforcement goals may bias the judgment of police officers in potentially dangerous ways and may contribute to aggressive or oppressive police conduct. Some jurisdictions have banned the use of quotas for traffic tickets.[37] Mandating a certain level of enforcement activity drives up the costs of policing for society and, therefore, reduces the "bottom line." There may be smarter ways, more economical with respect to the use of force or authority, to procure the compliance or behavioral changes sought.

Some departments deny setting quotas but admit to using enforcement productivity as a measure of patrol officers' effort; in other words, as a performance metric. In terms of the effect on police operations, the two ideas are virtually indistinguishable. Measures of overall productivity spanning the full range of patrol tasks (including but not limited to enforcement) can reveal over time who is working hard and who is not. That, of course, is important management information.

The danger of setting goals specifically for enforcement actions is that it may incline officers to stretch the limits of legality and fairness for the sake of another arrest or ticket. It is liable to produce quantity without regard to quality, relevance, or side effects. It undermines the importance of discretion and judgment exercised at the front line.

Despite these general cautions, the use of some kind of enforcement campaign might still be appropriate in specific circumstances, but the need would arise only when a specific type of enforcement focus has been selected as the solution to address a specific crime problem. All of the following conditions would need to be satisfied:

- A specific pattern of crime is being addressed.
- The problem has been properly analyzed.
- All the intervention options have been given full and open-minded consideration.
- An action plan has been chosen that requires a period of intensive enforcement attention to specific violations (which we might call an enforcement campaign).
- Instructions to frontline officers make it clear that, despite the context, every enforcement action must, given the circumstances of the case, be legally justifiable and appropriate.
- During the implementation of the plan, management constantly and carefully monitors the legality, reasonableness, relevance, impact, and side effects of the enforcement activities, so that operations can wind down or change course as soon as is appropriate.

In this context, the use of a functional focus fits Behn's managerial purposes of control (to make sure employees are carrying out the plan), and motivation (to increase intensity of effort).

But the plan being carried out is one thoughtfully designed in response to a specific crime problem. The campaign is appropriate, therefore, because it constitutes an intervention for a specific problem. This differs from setting enforcement quotas just because "that's what we do to show we're serious" or because particular executives have an ideological preference for certain types of activity. A wise craftsman does not "believe in" any one tool any more than any other. Enforcement campaigns should be used seldom; and their occasional use should be thoughtful, carefully monitored, and temporary.

If unrelenting pressure is applied to police officers to meet activity quotas of any kind (enforcement related or not), they will surely find ways to produce quantity, even at the expense of quality, relevance, appropriateness, or their own better judgment. If the goals set are unreasonable or not achievable through legitimate means, then illegitimate means may well be employed, producing behaviors not in the public interest.

As Andrew P. Scipione, commissioner of police in New South Wales, Australia, wrote in 2012:

> There is a delicate balance. A preoccupation with numbers is unhealthy if it distracts from the primary need to apprehend the most serious criminals and care for the most traumatized victims; it is unhealthier still if it causes police on the streets to set aside sound judgment and the public good in the pursuit of arrest quotas, lest they attract management criticism or compromise their chances of promotion.[38]

What about setting process-based goals? For core processes it rarely makes sense to set goals for the incoming volume of transactions, as that is not usually under the organization's control. It is appropriate to set goals for timeliness in processing, accuracy in determinations, and client satisfaction. All three of these are candidates for close-to-real-time monitoring and target setting.

But managers should be careful to adjust the balance between them, as too great an emphasis on timeliness can end up damaging accuracy and client satisfaction.

It is both appropriate and necessary to pay serious attention to cost efficiency in high-volume processes. But efficiency gains are best achieved by periodically rethinking or redesigning the underlying processes (using technology and business process improvement methods) rather than by exerting constant pressure on operational staff. Pressing staff to minimize costs or increase throughput is likely to undermine accuracy.

What about setting goals for risk-based work? Executives should demand vigilance from their crime analysis and intelligence staff, so that their department spots emerging problems earlier rather than later. Executives should demand nimbleness and fluidity from those responsible for allocating resources within the system, so that the right set of players can be formed into the right kind of team, at the right level, to tackle each unique pattern of crime or harm that appears. In addition, executives can emphasize their expectations for creativity and skill from those to whom problem-solving projects are entrusted.

Those involved in risk-based (problem-oriented) work should retain a strong methodological focus on achieving relevant outcomes rather than churning out enormous volumes of familiar outputs. It is tempting, once a plausible plan has been selected that involves activities, to allow the monitoring systems to focus on the production of those activities rather than achievement of the desired outcomes. What starts as thoughtful risk-based work can morph over time into functional quotas—not least because functional quotas are much easier to monitor.

A Closer Look at Crime Reduction as the Bottom Line of Policing

Holding these broader frameworks in mind, let us return for a moment to the dangers of relying too heavily on reported crime rates as the bottom line for policing. More needs to be said about the ways in which a relentless focus on reductions in reported crime rates (1) produces too narrow a focus, and (2) invites manipulation of statistics and other forms of corruption.

The Dangers of Narrowness

The focus is narrow because crime control is just one of several components of the police mission. The focus on serious crimes is narrower still, as community concerns often revolve around other problems. The focus on aggregate numbers is misleading, as some crimes have a disproportionate impact on community life or levels of fear.

Focusing on reported crime overlooks unreported crimes, which are generally more numerous than reported crimes. Particular types of crime—sexual assaults, domestic violence and other crimes within the family, white-collar crimes, crimes involving intimidation or where victims have a reason not to want to go to the authorities—are notoriously underreported. Klockars points out that even homicide rates may be unreliable to a degree.[39] Apparent suicides, deaths reported as accidental, and unresolved cases of missing persons all may act as masks for some murders. "Particularly vulnerable to having their murders misclassified this way are transients, street people, illegal aliens, and others who, if missed at all, are not missed for long."[40] Consensual crimes (such as bribery or drug dealing), with no immediate victim to complain, go essentially unreported and, therefore, appear in police statistics only if they are uncovered through police operations.

Most commentators recognize the difficulty and expense of carrying out victimization surveys to get better estimates. But most find no available alternative and recommend police departments consider the option seriously. As Moore and colleagues put it:

Determining the level of *unreported crime* is important not only to get a more accurate measure of the real rate of criminal victimization, but also to determine how much confidence citizens have in asking the police for help.

The only way to measure the underlying rate of victimization is to conduct a general survey of citizens asking about their victimization and their reasons for failing to report crime to the police. . . . If one wants to get close to the real level of victimization, and to learn about the extent to which the police have earned citizens' confidence in responding to criminal offenses, then there is little choice but to complement information on reported crime with information gained from general surveys of local populations.[41]

Moore and his coauthors also note the efficiencies available once a system for conducting victimization surveys has been set up. "We can use that system to *answer many other important questions about policing.* Specifically, we can learn a great deal about citizens' fears and their self-defense efforts, as well as their criminal victimization. We can learn about their general attitudes toward the police and how those attitudes are formed."[42]

Moore and Braga also point out the value of using other data sources as a way of cross-checking or validating trends suggested by police statistics. Particularly useful would be public health data from hospital emergency rooms that might reveal "the physical attacks that happen behind closed doors, or which are otherwise not reported to the police."[43] Langton and colleagues estimate that, nationwide, 31 percent of victimizations from

2006 to 2010 involving a weapon and injury to the victim went unreported to police.[44] Even when assaults involved the use of a firearm, roughly four in ten cases went unreported to police.[45] Many such cases are visible to public health systems.

As noted earlier, pressure to reduce the numbers is counterproductive when dealing with the whole class of invisible crimes (classically unreported or underreported crimes). Successful campaigns against these types of crime often involve deliberate attempts to expose the problem by first driving reporting rates up, not down.[46]

Corruption in Reporting Crime Statistics

Relentless pressure to reduce the number of crimes reported, without equivalent pressure to preserve the integrity of the recording and reporting systems, invites manipulation of statistics. The most obvious forms of manipulation involve suppression of reports (failing to take reports of crime from victims), and misclassification of crimes to lower categories to make the serious crime statistics look better.

This ought not to surprise anyone. It is an obvious danger naturally produced by too narrow a focus on one numerical metric. John A. Eterno and Eli B. Silverman, in their 2012 book, *The Crime Numbers Game*: *Management by Manipulation*, have compiled an extensive history of corruption scandals involving manipulation of crime statistics that spans decades and many countries. England and Wales, France, and the Australian Territories of New South Wales and Victoria have all experienced major scandals.[47] In the 1980s the Chicago Police Department suffered a major scandal, accused of "killing crime" on a massive scale by refusing to write up official reports of offenses reported to them.[48] Detectives were caught "unfounding" (determining a case was unverifiable) complaints of rape, robbery, and assault without investigation.[49] Other major U.S. cities have had similar scandals, including Baltimore, Washington, D.C., New York City,[50] Atlanta, and Boca Raton.[51]

Cheating on crime statistics, as a formidable temptation for police departments, goes with the territory. It remains a current problem, with a continuing stream of allegations and inquiries in various jurisdictions. In the United Kingdom, Chief Inspector of Constabulary Tom Windsor testified to a Commons committee in December 2013 that British police forces were undoubtedly manipulating crime statistics, and the question was only "where, how much, how severe?"[52] According to the *Guardian*, he later hinted that he thought the cheating might be on an "industrial" scale.[53]

Two investigative reports published by *Chicago Magazine* in April and May 2014 raised new questions about manipulation of crime statistics by the Chicago Police Department, including the downgrading of homicide cases.[54] In Scotland, the U.K. Statistics Authority rejected the government's claims to have achieved record low crime rates in August 2014 amid claims from retired police officers that crime figures had been manipulated "to present a more rosy picture of law and order to the public."[55]

Eterno and Silverman also show, through their survey of relevant public management literature, that such dangers are well understood in other fields and by now ought to be broadly recognized throughout the public sector.[56] In 1976, social psychologist Donald Campbell wrote: "The more any quantitative social indicator is used for social decision-making, the more subject it will be to corruption pressures and the more apt it will be to distort or corrupt the social processes it is intended to monitor."[57] Addressing the phenomenon of crime statistics in particular, Campbell notes:

> Crime rates are in general very corruptible indicators. For many crimes, changes in rates are a reflection of changes in

the activity of the police rather than changes in the number of criminal acts. . . . It seems to be well documented that a well-publicized, deliberate effort at social change—Nixon's crackdown on crime—had as its main effect the corruption of crime-rate indicators . . . achieved through under-recording and by downgrading the crimes to less serious classifications.[58]

Diane Vaughan, who has studied organizational misconduct more broadly, observes: "When the achievement of the desired goals received strong cultural emphasis, while much less emphasis is placed on the norms regulating the means, these norms tend to lose their power to regulate behavior."[59]

What I have elsewhere termed performance-enhancing risk taking turns out to be one of the most common sources of public-sector corruption. Officials take actions that are illegal, unethical, or excessively risky, and they do so not because they are inherently bad people or motivated by personal gain, but because they want to help their agency do better or look better and they are often placed under intense pressure from a narrow set of quantitative performance metrics.[60] (See box 2-2 for a summary description of the essential elements that comprise this type of organizational behavior.) As a consequence of the pressures, an internal culture emerges that celebrates those who "know what's required and are prepared to step up," whether that means torturing terror suspects to extract information, "testilying" to procure convictions, or cooking the books to achieve the crime reductions that executives demand.

Few in the police profession will need to be told how one might "cook the books." Robert Zink, the recording secretary of NYPD's Patrolmen's Benevolent Association, put it plainly in 2004:

Box 2-2. Performance-Enhancing Risks

The essential elements comprising performance-enhancing risks are as follows:

A core performance imperative that is unambiguous, tangible, highly visible, and emphasized as critical to organizational success.

Metrics related to this performance imperative that are objective, (usually) numerical, and available quickly and easily. These metrics grab and hold everybody's attention.

A reward system that recognizes the contribution of individuals or units to this core performance imperative, providing an incentive for them to engage with . . .

A set of behaviors that enhance, or that staff believe may enhance, their contribution to that core performance.

A set of ancillary risks produced by those behaviors, potentially harmful to the organization or to others. These might be regulatory or litigation risks (in the case of unlawful behavior), or other classes of risk, such as financial risk, reputational risks, or market risks.

The ancillary risks have uncertain, indirect, or longer-term consequences that allow individuals to discount potential damage, assume their behaviors will not be detected, hide behind ambiguity about the rules, and derive security from the presumption that the organization itself "doesn't want to know" how they meet performance expectations.

Inadequate countervailing pressures are in place to control those risky behaviors.

Source: Taken from Malcolm K. Sparrow, *The Character of Harms: Operational Challenges in Control* (Cambridge University Press, 2008), pp. 247–48.

So how do you fake a crime decrease? It's pretty simple. Don't file reports, misclassify crimes from felonies to misdemeanors, under-value the property lost to crime so it's not a felony, and report a series of crimes as a single event. A particularly insidious way to fudge the numbers is to make it difficult or impossible for people to report crimes—in other words, make the victims feel like criminals so they walk away just to spare themselves further pain and suffering.[61]

Integrity Issues Related to CompStat and Crime Reporting at the NYPD

There is good reason to pay special attention to the NYPD's early experience with CompStat. A great many other departments have copied it and now run similar systems or variants of it. The use of CompStat-style systems has substantially affected how many police departments view performance measurement, both in the ways they describe their performance at the agency level and in the ways they hold subunits accountable. So the effects of such systems—both positive and negative—need to be broadly understood.

The original form of CompStat, as implemented by the NYPD in 1994, had a set of very particular features. The system focused almost exclusively on reported rates for Part 1 Index crimes.[62] The principal data source was "reported crime," and the performance focus was unambiguously and always to "drive the numbers down." Crime analysis was principally based on place and time, so that hot spots could be identified and dealt with. Accountability for performance was organized geographically and by precinct, and was, therefore, intensely focused on precinct commanders. The precinct commanders were required to stand and deliver their results, or explain the lack of them, at the "podium" in the CompStat meetings—a famously stressful experience.

The managerial style employed seemed combative and adversarial. Garry McCarthy, who experienced the system in New York and replicated it in Chicago, recalled the New York experience of CompStat meetings in an interview with *Chicago Magazine*: "When I was a commander in New York, it was full contact," he said in 2012. "And if you weren't careful, you could lose an eye."[63]

The early days of CompStat also focused on a particular class of offenders and offenses, and promoted a somewhat standardized response. As Bratton wrote in 1999, "Intensive quality-of-life enforcement has become the order of the day in the NYPD."[64] The targets were disorganized street criminals, as Bratton noted: "In fact, the criminal element responsible for most street crime is nothing but a bunch of disorganized individuals, many of whom are not very good at what they do. The police have all the advantages in training, equipment, organization, and strategy." The primary intervention strategy was aggressive street-order maintenance. "We can turn the tables on the criminal element. Instead of reacting to them, we can create a sense of police presence and police effectiveness that makes criminals react to us."

The CompStat system was also used to drive enforcement quotas throughout the city for arrests, citations, and stops/searches, as well as to press senior management's demands for reductions in reported crime rates. There is no doubt that the system was effective in driving performance of the type chosen. As Bratton wrote, "Goals, it turns out, are an extremely important part of lifting a low-performing organization to higher levels of accomplishment and revitalizing an organizational culture."

In 2002 Moore described the early implementation of CompStat in the NYPD this way: "It was close to a strict liability system focused on outcomes. As a result, it is not surprising that the system ran a strong current through the department. Given that the system was consciously constructed to be behaviorally powerful, it becomes particularly important to know what it was motivating managers to do."[65]

Eterno and Silverman surveyed retired NYPD managers at or above the rank of captain to try to understand the effects of the CompStat system on the nature and extent of crime statistics manipulation. One of their survey findings was that respondents reported a diminished sense of pressure for integrity in reporting, even as CompStat imposed enormous pressure for crime reductions.[66]

Former NYPD commissioner William J. Bratton, in a 2010 *New York Times* op-ed column, sought to summarily dismiss Eterno and Silverman's survey results, claiming: "The notion that there has been widespread downgrading of felony crime under Compstat is way off base."[67] Bratton suggested that the high frequency with which retirees from the department had reported being aware of crime statistics manipulation may have arisen from "the rumor mill repeating the same handful of stories."[68]

Bratton confirmed, however, that the pressures imposed by the CompStat system on precinct commanders produced winners and losers. "Like any meritocracy, CompStat has its losers, but it has also helped many winners advance faster and be given more responsibility. No one ever said that policing was a pressure-free profession."[69] The "winners" (according to respondents in Eterno and Silverman's survey) were those precinct commanders who managed to produce the double-digit reductions in crime figures that senior management demanded, and the losers were those who did not.

Public concerns about what CompStat was motivating managers to do were heightened when the *Village Voice* published transcripts of Officer Adrian Schoolcraft's secretly recorded audiotapes of roll calls and other police meetings. In 2010 journalist Graham Rayman wrote five articles between May 4 and August 25 exploring the manipulation of crime statistics and the application of arrest and stop-and-frisk quotas used in Bedford-Stuyvesant's 81st Precinct in Brooklyn, as well as a 2012 follow-up article confirming the results of the investigation.[70]

In addition, 2010 saw the first wave of internal investigations within the NYPD for crime statistics manipulation. A department spokesman told the *New York Times* in February 2010 that Commissioner Raymond Kelly had disciplined four precinct commanders and seven other senior managers for downgrading crime reports.[71] In October 2010 the department disciplined the former commander of the 81st Precinct and four others for downgrading or refusing to take crime reports.[72]

In January 2011 Commissioner Kelly appointed a panel of three former federal prosecutors to examine NYPD's crime statistics recording and reporting practices, giving them three to six months to report.[73] Sadly, one of the three died while the panel was conducting its investigation, but the remaining two published the final report on April 8, 2013.[74]

The Crime Reporting Review (CRR) Committee acknowledged the danger of senior managers exerting pressure on subordinates to manipulate crime statistics and noted that there had been substantiated reports of manipulation in the past. They reported that the NYPD's own investigation of the 81st Precinct had "largely substantiated" Officer Schoolcraft's allegations regarding precinct supervisors exerting significant pressure on patrol officers not only to meet quotas on activity such as traffic tickets but also to manipulate or not take crime reports.

The CRR Committee had not been asked to determine the extent to which the NYPD had manipulated or was manipulating crime statistics. Rather, their task was to examine the control systems in place to see if they were robust enough to guarantee integrity in the face of the obvious and substantial pressures of the CompStat environment.

First, the committee examined the process-level controls and protocols governing the taking and classifying of crime reports. They determined that these were insufficient to counteract the danger of intentional manipulation. They then examined the audit systems that the NYPD used to review crime reports and crime classification decisions after the fact. They found, not surprisingly, that "the risk of suppression (as measured by its effect on reported crime) may be more substantial than the risk of downgrading."

With downgrading, there is at least a trail of records that can be reviewed, from the initial "scratch report" to the final system entry, and a set of policy criteria are available to test the determinations made. The system of audits conducted by the Quality Assurance Division (QAD) that the department used to test crime classifications uncovered patterns of downgrading with respect to robberies, burglaries, and larcenies. QAD audits identified patterns of larcenies downgraded to lost property when complainants did not see their property being stolen, robberies being downgraded to larcenies, burglaries being downgraded to larcenies by omitting a complaint of an unlawful entry, and attempted burglaries evidenced by broken locks or attempted breakdown of a door being classified as criminal mischief.

With crime suppression—failing to take a complaint, discouraging or intimidating a complainant, or otherwise making it awkward or unpleasant to report crime—there is often no written record to review, except in the case of 911 "radio runs" when the central call system retains a note of the original call. The most plausible way to detect patterns of suppression is to audit the radio runs and revisit the callers, comparing what happened within the department with what should have happened as a result of the call. The NYPD implemented such audits (called SPRINT audits) in 2010.

The CRR Committee noted that before 2010 no mechanisms were in place to determine the level of crime suppression; hence, there was no way of estimating the effect that any patterns of crime suppression may have had on NYPD's recorded crime rates. The committee also noted that implementation of the SPRINT audits had resulted in a relatively high rate of disciplinary actions, with investigations of seventy-one commands in 2011 and fifty-seven commands in 2012, and administrative sanctions being sought against 173 officers as a result of those investigations. The committee recommended a substantial increase in the breadth, depth, and volume of SPRINT audits in the future as, at the time of the committee's report (2013), these had been applied only to limited categories of calls (robbery and burglary).

Wesley Skogan points out that this type of audit, even if used extensively, can still only provide a partial view of crime suppression practices.[75] Sampling the transactions that pass through a centralized 911 system misses all the other attempts by citizens to report crimes through the panoply of alternate channels now available—beepers, cell phones, voice mail, and face-to-face reporting.[76]

Almost nobody denies that the relentless pressure to reduce reported (or, to be more precise, recorded) crime rates produced patterns of misclassification and crime report suppression. The question of the extent to which manipulation of crime statistics became institutionalized at NYPD, or whether the cases of manipulation that have come to light were isolated, remains unresolved. This chapter cannot and does not attempt to resolve that question.

Nobody doubts that crime has fallen dramatically in New York City in the last twenty years, and that the city is now much safer than it was before. The CRR Committee was keen to make that clear, noting in its conclusion that declines in overall crime rates in NYC over the previous ten or twenty years were, indeed, "historic."[77] The purpose here is not to undermine the achievements of the NYPD. CompStat was a major innovation when it was introduced and no doubt contributed substantially to the crime rate reductions achieved, even though criminologists still disagree about how much.[78]

There is evidence that the NYPD has recognized some of the dangers of its original CompStat model. The NYPD has disciplined a substantial number of officers over issues of crime suppression and misclassification and increased the number and types of audits designed to help guarantee integrity in reporting. Precinct-level officers interviewed by the CRR Committee during the review period, 2011–13, indicated that "the culture surrounding complaint-reporting had changed [improved] from 'what it had been.'"[79] The NYPD has also backed off its use of enforcement quotas to some degree. These are signs that the NYPD is rebalancing the pressures acting on its officers and paying more attention to the means as well as to the ends of reducing reported crime rates.

Looking forward, and with a focus on best practice, I stress that intense pressure for a reduction in crime numbers is liable—for many reasons well understood throughout private industry and in public management—to produce corruption, manipulation of statistics, and other patterns of behavior not in the public interest unless an equivalent and counterbalancing level of attention is paid to the integrity of recording and reporting systems, the governance of means, and careful monitoring of side effects. Even departments that do great work, if they leave themselves exposed to integrity risks, may face public cynicism about their self-reported results and an ugly cloud hanging over their successes.

Implications for CompStat-Like Systems

There has been much debate as to whether the early focus of CompStat and the methods that the system drove were ever right, even for New York City. The 1999 collection of essays, *Measuring What Matters*,[80] reflects much of that debate. But that particular form of CompStat is not appropriate now, and certainly is not appropriate in general or in other jurisdictions.

In the last twenty years the police profession has had the opportunity to learn a great deal about the strengths and weaknesses of the original CompStat model, and to figure out what types of modifications to the original model can improve it or better adapt it for use in other jurisdictions. Many variations can now be found. Some of them still reflect the narrow focus of the original form. Other versions are much broader, more mature, and seem both more versatile and, in some ways, more humane. Which version a department uses is likely to have a significant effect on its approach to performance measurement and reporting.

Table 2-2 shows six dimensions in which CompStat-like systems for crime analysis and accountability might be either narrower or broader. These six dimensions provide an opportunity for police executives to examine their own system and determine where, along each spectrum, their current CompStat implementation lies. Any dimension in which a system sits close to the narrow end represents an opportunity for improvement, and might enable a department to replace its current model with a more versatile and less restrictive version.

Many of the issues discussed so far in this chapter would naturally push toward the broader end of each spectrum. Recognizing Goldstein's more inclusive view of the police mission, Moore's multiple dimensions of performance, and the need for organizational nimbleness and skill in addressing many differ-

TABLE 2-2. CompStat Implementation Options		
	Narrow forms	Broader (mature) forms
Data sources	Reported crime rates	Multiple sources, including victimization surveys
Forms of analysis	Geographic (by precinct and cluster) and temporal	Versatile, considering full range of relevant dimensions
Performance focus	Drive the numbers down	Emphasize increased reporting to expose and deal with hidden problems
Locus of responsibility	Precinct commanders	Tailored to each problem
Managerial style	Adversarial	Cooperative/coaching
Preferred tactics	Directed patrol, street order maintenance	Full range of interventions

ent types of problems that police face should all help to shake police departments out of too narrow a focus.

Data Sources

As this chapter has already made clear, Part 1 Index crimes remain important, but community concerns frequently center on other issues. Many crimes are not reported, and, therefore, police would need to use a broader range of data sources—including public health information and victimization surveys—even to be able to see the full range of problems that matter.

Forms of Analysis

Crime analysis should no longer revolve solely or mainly around hot spot analysis. Goldstein repeatedly pressed police to recognize that crime problems were often not concentrated geographically but in other dimensions (for example, repeat offenders who roamed the city, repeat victims, methods of commission, patterns of behavior, and types of victims).[81] Therefore, adding forms of analysis that focus on dimensions other than time and place is important for broadening the range of problems that crime analysis can reveal.

Performance Focus

The performance focus should be carefully chosen, depending on the character of the problem being addressed. "Driving numbers down" is an appropriate focus only for crimes where discovery rates are high and the frequency of the crime is currently far greater than normal levels (that is, there is slack to be taken up). It is not appropriate for the many types of invisible problems that need to be better exposed before they can be dealt with. And "reducing the numbers" will not be possible in perpetuity, as crime rates will inevitably level off once they have reached reasonable levels. For jurisdictions that are relatively safe to begin with, reductions may not be possible even in the short term.

Locus of Responsibility

It makes sense to make precinct commanders unambiguously responsible for problems that are tightly concentrated within one precinct. But many issues are citywide or fit awkwardly into the precinct structure. A mature problem-oriented organization will use more fluid systems that allow for the formation of problem-solving teams at many different organizational levels to match the breadth and distribution of various problems.

Managerial Style

In terms of managerial style, pressure to perform is one thing, but a modern police department has no place for tyrannical management, deliberate humiliation of officers in front of their peers, or attempts to catch them out with analytic findings not previously shared. Mature forms of CompStat should embody congenial and cooperative managerial relationships even as they remain ruthlessly analytical and outcome oriented. Adversarial managerial styles exercised at high levels within a department tend to trickle all the way down, resulting in intolerable pressure on front line officers and, ultimately, inappropriate forms of police action on the streets.

Preferred Tactics

Aggressive zero-tolerance–style policing is relevant only to specific classes of street crime and, as many commentators have observed, can destroy community relationships and cooperation. Persistent use of aggressive policing tactics, particularly in disadvantaged and minority neighborhoods, may be a recipe for anti-police riots in the end, given some appropriate spark. A mature CompStat system should bring no underlying preference for any particular set of tactics. Teams working on problems should be required and expected to consider the full range of interventions available to them, and to invent new methods where necessary.

Conclusion

The principal purpose of this chapter has been to highlight some of the narrower traditions into which police organizations fall when describing their value and reporting their performance. A modern police organization needs a broader view of its mission (per Goldstein),[82] a broader view of the dimensions of performance (per Moore),[83] and a clear understanding of the metrics that go with different types of work. Overall, police departments need more complex cockpits. Police executives need a more sophisticated understanding of how to use different types of information to understand the condition of their organizations and what is happening in the communities they serve.

Another purpose of this chapter was to point police executives toward useful resources on this subject. For those interested in developing a more comprehensive suite of instruments for their "cockpit" and a clearer sense of how to use them all, I particularly recommend the sections referenced in the "Recommended Further Readings" at the end of this chapter as relevant, practical, and accessible.

In discussing this subject with police executives in the classroom, two questions invariably come up. First, someone will object. "So what's new? Haven't you just invented the balanced scorecard for public agencies?"

Not exactly. The cockpit I imagine is not really a "balanced scorecard." It is hardly a scorecard at all. It is a richer information environment with much more sophisticated users. Police executives need a more comprehensive suite of managerial information but—like the airline pilot—should be slow to label any specific dial a performance indicator. As soon as you designate an indicator as a performance indicator, you need to think carefully about the currents that will run through the organization and make sure you anticipate and can control perverse behaviors that may arise.

The second question students raise is this: "So, to get the public and the politicians to pay attention to this broader, more complex performance story, should we withhold the traditional statistics (reported Part 1 crime figures) so we are not held hostage by them?"

My normal advice is basically this: "No, it's a democracy, and transparency is the default setting. You cannot and would not want to hide that information. It remains important managerial information. Your job is not to withhold the traditional performance account, but to dethrone it. You have to provide a richer story that better reflects the breadth of your mission and the contributions your agency makes. You have to provide that story even if the press, the politicians, and the public do not seem to be asking for it just yet. Educate them about what matters, by giving it to them whether they ask for it or not. In the end, you can reshape their expectations."

Box 2-3. **Recommended Further Reading**

In *Measuring What Matters* (pp. 43–47), Wesley Skogan provides a practical discussion of methods for assessing levels of disorder in neighborhoods.[a]

In *Measuring What Matters* (pp. 47–50), Skogan offers advice on measuring the fear of crime and its impact on community behavior and the use of public spaces.[b]

In *Measuring What Matters* (pp. 58–59), Darrel Stephens offers ideas about measuring disorder and describes work by volunteer groups in St. Petersburg to survey residents and record physical conditions in neighborhoods.[c]

In *Measuring What* Matters (pp. 202–04), Carl Klockars provides examples of simple-to-administer crime victim surveys, asking for feedback on the nature and quality of services delivered to them by police departments.[d]

In *Measuring What Matters* (pp. 208–12), Klockars stresses the importance of assessing levels of integrity within a police department (as a matter of organizational culture, rather than trying to measure actual levels of corruption) and describes some practical ways of doing what many might claim cannot be done.[e]

In *The "Bottom Line" of Policing* (pp. 30–75), in a section titled "Measuring Performance on the Seven Dimensions," Mark Moore and Anthony Braga provide a rich collection of practical ways to gather data, use existing data, and generate indicators relevant to each of the seven dimensions of performance. These are summarized in note form in table 3 (pp. 80–82) with suggestions for immediate investments prioritized in table 4 (pp. 83–85).[f]

Chapter 8 of *The Character of Harms* explores the special challenges that go with the class of invisible risks (those with low discovery rates). Much of that discussion revolves around issues of measurement, in particular the methods required to resolve the inherent ambiguity of readily available metrics.[g]

The 2012 Bureau of Justice Statistics special report, *Victimizations Not Reported to the Police, 2006–2010,* by Lynn Langton and others, provides an interesting and data-rich analysis of the frequencies with which various forms of victimization are not reported to the police.[h]

Chapter 12 of *The Character of Harms* provides a more rigorous analysis of performance-enhancing risks, describing the special threats to integrity that commonly arise when too much emphasis is placed on too narrow a set of quantitative metrics.[i]

Notes

a. *Measuring What Matters: Proceedings from the Policing Research Institute Meetings,* edited by Robert H. Langworthy. Research Report (Washington, D.C.: U.S. Department of Justice, National Institute of Justice, July 1999), NCJ 170610.
b. Ibid.
c. Ibid.
d. Ibid.
e. Ibid.
f. Mark H. Moore and Anthony Braga, *The "Bottom Line" of Policing: What Citizens Should Value (and Measure!) in Police Performance* (Washington, D.C.: Police Executive Research Forum, 2003)
g. Malcolm K. Sparrow, *The Character of Harms: Operational Challenges in Control* (Cambridge University Press, 2008).
h. Lynn Langton and others, *Victimizations Not Reported to the Police, 2006–2010.* Special Report (Washington, D.C.: U.S. Department of Justice, Bureau of Justice Statistics, August 2012), NCJ 238536.
i. Sparrow, *The Character of Harms.*

THREE

What Happened to Community and Problem-Oriented Policing?

How could it be that Department of Justice investigators, in 2015, recommended the Ferguson Police Department implement community and problem-oriented policing, ideas that seemed well established as the basis for police reform as early as the 1980s and 1990s? It was not that the Ferguson Police Department had never heard of these ideas. Rather, their current practices revealed little attention to or formal investment in these ideas:

> Ferguson's community policing efforts appear always to have been somewhat modest, but have dwindled to almost nothing in recent years. FPD has no community policing or community engagement plan. FPD currently designates a single officer the "Community Resource Officer." This officer attends community meetings, serves as FPD's public relations liaison, and is charged with collecting crime data. No other officers play any substantive role in community policing efforts.[1]

Police officers in Ferguson acknowledged that the department's focus on raising revenue had helped to displace the mission and values of community policing. Also, administrative changes (such as adoption of twelve-hour shifts) made in support of traffic enforcement priorities made it harder for officers to establish or maintain meaningful relationships with the community.[2]

In this respect, therefore, the Ferguson Police Department may not be atypical. They, like virtually everyone else in policing, had heard of the ideas of community and problem-oriented policing. They had implemented some version of community policing, once upon a time. But the department's mission and methods no longer revolved around the ideals of community and problem-oriented policing. What was left, in terms of operational implementation, was a mere token.

Anthony Braga, in his 2015 Perspectives series paper "Crime and Policing Revisited,"[3] reports that such tokenism appears widespread:

> Even though community problem-solving policing concepts are now ubiquitous in the policing profession, the experiences of the police executives in the [Executive Session on Policing and Public Safety], coupled with the available literature on implementation, suggest that many police departments are not embracing these approaches with fidelity to the original ideas. For instance, the available research suggests that community policing has been unevenly implemented within police departments, with responsibility for community-based initiatives sometimes relegated to specialized units composed of a small number of officers rather than spread across police departments. . . . Police officers also often find it difficult to implement problem-oriented policing properly with deficiencies existing in all stages of the process, resulting in an over-reliance on traditional policing tactics. . . . Too many police

departments seem to rely on over-simplistic tactics, such as "putting cops on dots" or launching indiscriminate zero-tolerance initiatives rather than engaging a coherent crime prevention strategy.[4]

According to Braga, the original ideas have held up to scholarly scrutiny, with sufficient evidence now available to support the conclusion that "the police can reduce crime if they take a focused approach to addressing recurring crime problems, engage the community and a diversity of partners, and implement tactics and strategies appropriately tailored to the conditions that give rise to crime problems."[5] But that only deepens the mystery. If these ideas are demonstrably effective when properly implemented, why would the profession's adoption of them remain so half-hearted and patchy?

That is the work for this chapter. There are many reasons. One of them, for sure, is the proliferation of *other* ideas that, in the minds of practitioners, compete for attention with community and problem-oriented policing.

The Proliferation of Ideas

In various executive training classes over the last few years, I have asked senior police managers to list the policing strategies and/or theories that have helped to shape their departments' operations. I ask them to include only those that have some concrete operational embodiment within their departments, and, thereby, exclude ideas adopted as mere rhetoric. The list they produce is impressive, and many executives report that their departments use as many as four or five different strategies simultaneously. For many practitioners the relationship between these ideas seems unclear. For some, the proliferation of what they jokingly refer to as "hyphenated policing" creates enormous confusion.

The strategies most commonly named are:

- Community policing
- Neighborhood-oriented policing
- Problem-oriented policing
- Broken Windows policing
- Zero-Tolerance policing
- Hot-spots policing
- Situational crime control
- Intelligence-led policing
- Predictive policing
- CompStat
- Evidence-based policing

Police departments across the United States vary in how many of these approaches they have embraced, and which combinations. Moreover, implementation of any one of these strategies varies enormously from jurisdiction to jurisdiction and over time. As implementations mature they tend to become more versatile and better adapted to local circumstances, departing from more standardized models that were originally imported or copied from other jurisdictions.

This is not the place to provide a complete history or exposition of each of these ideas. But it may be worthwhile here to reduce them to their bare bones, for two purposes: first, to clarify the distinctions between them (for the sake of readers not fully conversant with them) and, second, to open up the space *between* these ideas, so police executives can develop a clear sense of the dangers of standardized and formulaic implementations, which tend to be narrow in scope and suitable only for certain categories of problems. This should enable police executives to explore *what else* they might need, in addition to their existing methods of operation, to support effective action across the full range of police tasks.

What is striking about the list is how many of these are reduced forms of community or problem-oriented policing. That is, they reflect attempts to implement these foundational ideas but, to make them practical, particular choices were made that narrowed the focus in one way or another and led to an operational implementation that is relatively inflexible.

Neighborhood-oriented policing (NOP) was, in the 1980s and 1990s, almost synonymous with community-oriented policing (COP). Both NOP and COP signaled close cooperation with local communities in agenda setting and in coproduction of public safety. With the passage of time, the term *neighborhood-oriented policing* lost out, and community-oriented policing, or just community policing, became the more common terminology.

If there were any difference between NOP and COP, it would be that NOP focused on a particular type of community: those defined at the level of the neighborhood. There are other "communities" as well—including business communities, citywide communities, and regional communities—that can make quite proper claims on police attention. One interesting question to ask of a department that claims to operate community-oriented policing is "what types of communities do you recognize and focus upon?" Answers will vary, but neighborhood communities remain at the top of the priority list for most departments seriously committed to COP.

Six strategies on the list (Broken Windows policing, Zero-Tolerance policing, hot-spots policing, situational crime control, intelligence-led policing, and predictive policing) turn out, on close examination, to be reduced forms of problem-oriented policing. That is, they are designed to address specific types of crime problems, or to address crime patterns in particular ways. They are each *particular* in some respect, where problem-oriented policing was intended to be quite *general*.

Broken Windows policing and Zero-Tolerance policing tend to go hand in hand, as most famously implemented by the NYPD. Broken Windows names the theory and ostensibly connects to relevant research. Zero tolerance describes the dominant operational focus—aggressive enforcement of minor infractions—justified, at least in the eyes of proponents, by the Broken Windows theory. This strategy is particular and restrictive in the sense that it constitutes a standardized approach to crime control by establishing default intervention tactics. Problem-oriented policing, by contrast, never establishes default tactics but demands that careful analysis of specific problems be followed by a genuine search for tailor-made solutions, drawing from a much richer collection of potential interventions and frequently inventing new and unique approaches.

Hot-spots policing, as its name suggests, focuses on patterns of crime that are concentrated in space and time. Some crime problems are concentrated that way, but many are not. One of Herman Goldstein's initial pleas to the police profession when introducing his notion of problem-oriented policing was that they should learn to recognize the many other dimensions in which crime problems might be concentrated: by repeat offender, or repeat victim, by a class of offenders, by a class of victims, by a crime method, by season, by motive, and so on. Police, he said, have *always* concentrated on hot spots, even before the advent of computerized analysis, using pin-maps on the precinct commander's office wall.

So hot-spots policing can be useful to address a particular subset of problems, namely those that have a geographic concentration. Of course, there is nothing wrong with this approach, providing its limitations are recognized and understood.

Hot-spots policing has received a considerable degree of scholarly attention lately, and has matured in some respects from its legacy versions. Prior to Goldstein, not only was the form of analysis standardized (geographic and temporal clustering), but so was the tactical response. Directed patrol was the default response, which meant flooding the relevant area with police at the relevant times (affectionately known as putting "cops on dots"). Recent work has broadened the range of responses to hot spots, and some of those approaches involve local residents and businesses in helping to deal with the problems. In other words, the range of intervention methods has broadened. Greater precision in analytical and mapping techniques has also supported disaggregation of crime concentrations to lower levels, even to the level of specific city blocks, stretches of road, or intersections.

Situational crime control focuses on one particular mode of intervention: reducing the availability of places suitable or convenient for crime. Ron Clarke, one of the leading proponents, describes it thus:

> Situational crime prevention . . . refers to a pre-emptive approach that relies, not on improving society or its institutions, but simply on reducing the opportunities for crime. . . . Situational crime prevention comprises opportunity-reducing measures that are (1) directed at highly specific forms of crime, (2) involve the management, design, or manipulation of the immediate environment in as specific and permanent a way as possible, (3) so as to increase the effort and risks of crime and reduce the rewards as perceived by a wide range of offenders.[6]

Goldstein persistently encourages police to keep their minds open to the full range of problems, the full range of dimensions in which problems might be concentrated, and the full range

of intervention techniques. So he welcomes situational prevention, but points to its limitations: "Clarke identified sixteen
techniques of situational prevention. Problem-oriented policing
would embrace all of these—but, in its concern for the range of
community problems that the police must handle beyond crime,
embrace many additional strategies as well."[7]

Intelligence-led policing (ILP) focuses on problems of particular shapes. The most common focus is on repeat offenders,
so the analytic and intelligence work that supports ILP tends
to be offender-centric, connecting crimes committed by prolific
and dangerous criminals. The modes of intervention naturally
follow the offender-centric theme of ILP, and include a range of
methods for monitoring and controlling the behavior of persistent offenders.

Varieties of ILP exist, some of them including types of crime
concentration in addition to those characterized as the work
of repeat offenders. The British National Intelligence Model,
for instance, is set up to identify and deal with serious offenders as well as crime and disorder hot spots, organized crime,
and "series" crimes such as those involving a common victim or
method.[8]

Predictive policing is a more recent addition to the list of
police strategies, and it is not yet entirely clear how much this
idea differs from better-established ideas. The predictive policing label has been used in two quite different ways. One relates to long-term strategic planning, whereby police executives
engage with city planners and demographers to specify policing needs five or ten years into the future and plan accordingly.
The second (much more common) version relates to a class of
analytic methods designed to predict when and where crime is
likely to occur. Those methods involve pattern recognition applied to historical data and then extrapolated into the future.
For anyone familiar with crime analysis, that is not new. And

it's particularly not new when the default intervention strategy involves putting cops on dots.

David Sklansky observes the strong tendency for police technology to be overhyped, and comments: "For all the talk about 'advanced analytics' and 'data fusion' that can 'discover nonobvious relationships' among risk factors for crime, the proven successes of predictive policing have involved fairly prosaic techniques."[9]

Many of those successes, so far, have involved spatial and temporal analysis to spot existing concentrations, leading to the default response of directed patrol. Such implementations seem little more than a continuation of hot-spots policing but under a different name.

If predictive policing provides little that is genuinely new, one wonders why it deserves a new name. The answer, Sklansky proposes, is simple and results from the existence of a commercial market in predictive analytics, which extends beyond policing and has targeted government agencies quite broadly:[10] "Part of the reason technology tends to be over-hyped is that there is money to be made from selling it. Another part of the reason is simply that gear and gadgets are sexy: shiny video screens, interactive maps, and 'mathematical prophesy' have allures that are not shared by, say, a poorly attended community meeting in a church basement."[11]

Given the advent of richer data and greater computational power, it is quite plausible that predictive policing will, in fact, provide the police profession with finer-grained and, therefore, more precise analyses than those previously available. But here one cannot help but observe the tendency of the police profession when offered beefed-up analytic capabilities: they tend to use new technology to refine those analytic methods with which they are already deeply familiar and comfortable, but they lack the imagination to break out of old habits and broaden their analytic repertoire. Sklansky echoes this worry, and describes how one sociologist, Peter K. Manning, "spent six years watching the use of crime mapping and information technology in management meetings in three U.S. police departments [and] concluded that the data were almost never used to call existing strategies into question; for the most part, information technology was simply 'adapted to the police organization and its characteristic practices.'"[12]

CompStat systems incorporate aspects of crime analysis, performance measurement, and performance management. Implementations vary enormously in their maturity and versatility. The narrower forms, as discussed in detail in chapter 2, tend to focus heavily on reported crime rates for Part I offenses, rely on spatial and temporal analysis to spot clusters, place responsibility for interventions firmly at the level of precinct command, and, in some departments, assume a default treatment in the form of aggressive street order maintenance. More mature forms of CompStat are more versatile, drawing on multiple data sources, incorporating greater versatility in analytic and detection methods, and embracing a fuller range of potential interventions.

Evidence-based policing (EBP) describes one particular form of interaction between research and practice. Described by proponents as analogous to evidence-based medicine, the EBP movement focuses on establishing "what works" in policing—which means, more precisely, "which programs work." EBP relies heavily on statistical analysis and program-evaluation techniques, holding out randomized controlled trials as the gold standard for determining the extent to which various outcomes (including crime reductions) can be properly attributed to specific police strategies and tactics.

Most of the champions of EBP are criminologists or social scientists who work with police departments to design and conduct experiments to test one crime control strategy or another. One fundamental tenet of the EBP movement is that police ought not to be allowed to use programs or methods that have not been proven effective.

Chapter 4 examines in detail the degree to which EBP can support the maturing of problem-oriented policing. It concludes that EBP does indeed have a place within policing research, and that its methods are relevant in evaluating programs that are large, expensive, relatively permanent, and implemented across multiple departments in a sufficiently standardized way that they can be evaluated using social science research tools.

However, chapter 4 also concludes that EBP, if given a central or dominant role in defining scholar/practitioner relationships, can substantially impede the work of operational problem solving. Many other forms of analysis are vital, too, and EBP can serve to narrow the focus to a specific category of analytic methods that constitute disciplinary norms for the social sciences but often fail to provide the requisite analytic support for operational policing.

Community Policing: Hiccups along the Way

It may be worth enumerating the various hiccups that have impeded the development of community policing. Several of these involve the substitution of reduced forms of community policing.

Reduced Form: Focus on Specific Tactics

The first involves departments that adopt specific tactics associated with community policing but miss the concept's deeper philosophical and cultural implications. For some departments community policing means little more than increasing the use of foot or bicycle patrols, or even painting the squad cars white to make them appear less threatening.

Reduced Form: Isolating Community Policing within Dedicated Units

The second involves the creation of community policing units, often quite small. While such units may provide a valuable service, the danger is that the very existence of such a unit may allow the remainder of the department to preserve its traditional philosophy as professional crime fighters and remain completely disconnected from or unaffected by the community policing philosophy.

The President's Task Force on 21st Century Policing emphasized the importance of an organization-wide commitment to community policing:

> Community policing must be a way of doing business by an entire police force, not just a specialized unit of that force. . . . Community policing cannot be a program, unit, strategy, or tactic. It must be the core principle that lies at the foundation of a police department's culture. . . . Testimony from a number of witnesses also made clear that hiring, training, evaluating, and promoting officers based on their ability and track record in community engagement—not just traditional measures of policing such as arrests, tickets, or tactical skills—is an equally important component of the successful infusion of community policing throughout an organization.[13]

Reduced Form: A One-Sided Deal

Some departments attempt to engage the community as "eyes and ears"; that is, to provide information to the police in support of their traditional crime-fighting role. The one-sided nature of this deal is what eventually renders it unsustainable. Communities will not participate for long unless they know their own concerns are being taken seriously and incorporated into policing priorities. A more mature community policing model must be a two-sided deal: police and public working together not only to achieve results, but also to set the agenda. The advantages to the community must be obvious and tangible.

The Impact of Counterterrorism

The events of September 11 and the subsequent emphasis on national security profoundly affected domestic policing in the United States. Many of the ways in which policing changed were probably unavoidable, and may be permanent. But in the context of a discussion of community policing, it is important to recognize the effects that the national security agenda has had on the ways in which police interact with local communities. It might be useful to contemplate quite carefully what might need to be done now to make sure the original vision for community policing does not get buried by competing concerns.

Many commentators regard the advent of the security agenda as disastrous for community policing. David Couper, for instance, writes: "That day [9/11] changed just about everything in policing. It changed our nation's police for the worst as they lost their essential role to protect the citizens and their rights. Rather they became caught up in 'homeland security,' outfitted themselves in robot-like body armor, and procured the latest chemical agents and military equipment."[14]

Others see greater symbiosis, recognizing the valuable role that established and positive community relationships can play in counterterrorism. Sklansky, for instance, observes:

> As it happens, the most important contributions that local police departments can make to homeland security probably depend on precisely the kinds of outreach, partnership, and low-tech, person-to-person trust-building stressed in community policing. Information cannot be collated, shared, or cross-tabulated until it is collected, and people are much more likely to speak frankly with police officers they know, have worked with, and trust. When a police officer goes to talk with, say, a local Arab-American leader, it helps if the officer has "met and assisted that leader before—protecting property, ironing out some administrative complexity, or ensuring his safe worship." If we want to prevent attacks from Islamic extremists, our most important allies will be found among moderate, mainstream Islamic Americans, and the way to gain their trust and cooperation is by working with them in precisely the ways emphasized by community policing.[15]

Thus Sklansky stresses the value of community interactions styled in the manner of community policing. But notice that the *purpose* is, nevertheless, quite different, focusing on the necessity of detecting extremists, preventing radicalization, and uncovering plots—which is very different from working with communities to identify and address their own public safety concerns. Moreover, the *communities of interest* might be different, with special attention paid to those neighborhoods deemed more likely to source violent extremism or provide support to foreign powers or terrorist organizations. So there will still be some tension between the agendas of community policing and national security, even if both benefit from a similar style of community interaction.

There will be tension anyway between local, regional, and national priorities. The rubber hits the road at the same level—ground level—regardless of the size of the vehicle. Local police departments, with limited time and resources, have obligations to deliver on agendas conceived locally, at the state level, regionally, and nationally. Increased emphasis on national security and counterterrorism surely shifts the local resource allocation priorities in the direction of national and regional agendas. So does the advent of other nonlocalized policing priorities such as cyber-crime, financial fraud, identity theft, and human trafficking.

The tension between the national security agenda and local policing priorities manifests itself also in the nature of the networks that local police departments recognize, belong to, and can be obligated by.

- Network 1: Criminal justice system: Police had always regarded themselves as one element of the criminal justice system, feeders of the court system and natural partners with prisons and probation and parole services. The unifying mission for this network was crime control; in particular, incapacitation and, to a lesser extent, rehabilitation of offenders.
- Network 2: Municipal government: The advent of community and problem-oriented policing brought a different network membership. Police now acted as a component of municipal government. Police recognized the special value they brought by being available to citizens twenty-four hours a day and seven days a week, and with a phone number that everyone knew. They adopted the role of broker for municipal services, frequently referring those in need and other concerned citizens to agencies such as youth services, recreation, sanitation, road maintenance,

public health, and social services. The unifying mission for this network was quality of life in the city. Police were often the first agency to implement a problem-oriented approach, but some municipalities then picked up this tactic and broadened the scope to cover issues of community concern beyond crime and to coordinate responses from multiple municipal departments.

- Network 3: National security: The national security agenda obliges police to engage with a third network, focused on counterterrorism, security, and intelligence. This network includes intelligence agencies, other security agencies, immigration, and regional fusion centers. It draws agencies at all levels of government together around the tasks of data gathering, intelligence analysis, surveillance, and intelligence sharing . . . all serving the purpose of reducing the threat of terrorism. The international nature of terrorist threats makes collaboration across borders essential, and thus de-emphasizes local policing priorities.

The prominence of the counterterrorism mission since 2001 has pushed policing right into the center of the tension between security and civil liberties. Local police should be (and usually are) much closer to the people than other members of any security coalition (for example, federal agencies), and are thus well placed to play a balancing role between competing priorities. The more police departments identify with the security and intelligence network, the less likely they may be to stand up for constitutional rights and civil liberties when these do, indeed, come into conflict with the national security agenda.

Reduced Form: The Substitution of Zero-Tolerance Policing

Adopting any particular default intervention strategy, as discussed above, constitutes a narrowing of the problem-oriented approach. Adopting aggressive street-order maintenance as the default intervention strategy also conflicts with the fundamental values of community policing. Charles H. Ramsey, commissioner of police in Philadelphia and cochair of the President's Task Force on 21st Century Policing, expresses this rather forcefully in his recent New Perspectives series paper, in which he reflects on the role that police played during the Holocaust:

> Of course, the term "zero tolerance" is quite in vogue today. Some people even suggest (quite mistakenly, I would argue) that zero tolerance and community policing are one and the same, or at least closely related. What worries me most about this is that the ideals of democracy are all about tolerance—tolerance for different people, different cultures, different viewpoints. In the name of zero tolerance, many police departments today crack down on nuisance crimes such as drinking in public and other minor misdemeanors and almost always choose underprivileged neighborhoods for this strategy. I certainly do not advocate drinking in public or any other disorderly or criminal behavior. But how many of us ask the questions: Why is this person an alcoholic to begin with? And why doesn't he or she have a home to live in?
>
> If we are to stand for any type of zero tolerance, it should be zero tolerance for the causes of crime and zero tolerance for the types of racist attitudes that led to the Holocaust seventy years ago and continue to feed hate crimes in our communities today. That is the type of "zero tolerance" we, as police officers, should be focusing on. What followed from

the zero tolerance policies in Nazi Germany was the denial of basic human rights and individual freedoms.[16]

If the defenders of Zero-Tolerance policing rely on the Broken Windows theory to justify the approach, they appear to be on shaky ground. Braga, Welsh, and Schnell have pulled together in a preliminary Campbell Review the available evidence regarding various methods for controlling disorder. It turns out that aggressive order maintenance strategies do not appear to generate significant crime reductions, whereas community and problem-oriented approaches designed to address underlying conditions of disorder have demonstrated some substantial crime reduction effects.[17]

Resurgence of the "Police Professionalism" Agenda

A very current threat to the development and maturing of community policing results from too heavy an emphasis on other aspects of police professionalism. Sklansky warns that many of the modern ideas now circulating—including intelligence-led and predictive policing—might once again focus police on "the vision of an elite corps of expert crime-fighters, acting independently but objectively and scientifically, to keep communities safe." This vision, he says, is a "false ideal" that ignores "most of what we learned about policing in the 1960s, 1970s, and 1980s."[18]

Some might imagine that such expressions of concern reflect an anti-technology or even anti-modern-management bias. Not so. Proponents of community policing have always recognized the value of technology, accountability, integrity, discipline, better training, national standards, and a host of other positive developments that might fall naturally under the umbrella label of "professionalism." But they argue that these other areas for development are more natural and more attractive for police (in particular those that have to do with technology and equipment); that there is only so much attention to go around; and that the real issue is *emphasis*. As Sklansky puts it, we need to focus attention on "the problems in policing that most deserve attention, not only because of their intrinsic importance but also because of their difficulty and their tendency to be neglected."[19]

One of the central lessons from the investigation of the Ferguson Police Department, properly identified by Department of Justice investigators, is that whatever else is happening with respect to the development of policing, we need a renewed and concerted emphasis on the work of implementing community policing. For all the reasons described above, this applies quite broadly across the policing profession. The need to stick with the task of implementing community policing is by no means an issue just for a few especially troubled departments.

Problem-Oriented Policing: Hiccups along the Way

The development of problem-oriented policing (POP) has, likewise, encountered a variety of obstacles along the way. Some of them have already been mentioned, and many of them involve reduced forms and simplistic substitutions of one kind or another. The temptation to reduce and simplify is perfectly understandable, because managing problems turns out to be organizationally awkward and intellectually demanding. It also requires a great many choices to be made and forms of discretion to be exercised that are unfamiliar and discomforting for officers and managers accustomed to more routine forms of work.

The underlying idea is straightforward enough. In reviewing the evolution of crime-control strategies over the last few decades, Anthony Braga traces the origins of problem-oriented policing to Goldstein's "simple and straightforward proposition":

In 1979, Herman Goldstein, a respected University of Wisconsin law professor and former aide to Chicago police superintendent O. W. Wilson, made a simple and straightforward proposition that challenged police officers to address problems rather than simply respond to incidents. According to Goldstein . . . behind every recurring problem there are underlying conditions that create it. Incident-driven policing never addresses these conditions; therefore, incidents are likely to recur. Answering calls for service is an important task and still must be done, but police officers should respond systematically to recurring calls for the same problem. In order for the police to be more efficient and effective, they must gather information about incidents and design an appropriate response based on the nature of the underlying conditions that cause the problem(s).[20]

The challenges of problem-oriented policing laid down by Herman Goldstein, and developed further by many others since, emphasized the uniqueness of individual problems; the need to disaggregate them into their component parts; a willingness to consider a broad range of dimensions and potential sizes in so doing; the need to define problems carefully and accurately, capturing and considering multiple perspectives on the problem; an open-minded search for tailor-made solutions; and a commitment to methodological rigor in evaluating outcomes.

If the idea is straightforward, implementation is anything but. One study conducted in 1996 examined the experience of police in England and Wales with the concept of problem-oriented policing. Police officers provided to the researchers a substantial list of reasons why POP had not "taken off" despite more than a decade of attempts to incorporate it into police operations. Here are the major reasons given:[21]

- There is no time for it. Police in Britain are already over-stretched.
- There is nothing new about it. POP is just a fancy way of describing what is delivered routinely anyway.
- POP is impossible. Real issues are so complex and deep-rooted that piecemeal problem-solving efforts cannot succeed.
- The police job is to *respond to incidents*. It is up to others to "solve problems."
- Policing in Britain is about crime and detection. Addressing other problems is for other agencies.
- British police culture is so deep-rooted and so wrapped up in crime detection that there can be no serious prospect of implementing POP.
- Objectives are set nationally, which leaves little room to pay attention to distinctive concerns of individual communities.
- Management structures are not well adapted to the "bottom up" approach that characterizes POP.

Many other regulatory agencies have experimented with equivalent ideas, even if they use slightly different vocabulary to describe them. Florida's Department of Environmental Protection, which implemented an environmental problem-solving program in the late 1990s, encountered similar challenges. A group of internal consultants designated to help drive the problem-solving program and provide support to project teams, after a couple of years of working on the program, listed reasons why, in their view, problem solving proved perpetually challenging. They echoed many of the objections raised by U.K. police, and added a few more:[22]

- The required analytic support (data analysis and help with statistical work) is not available.

- Problem solving has no formal budgetary support, nor any legislative mandate. Everything else the department does has both.
- Real-world problems come in awkward shapes and sizes that do not fit established groups or units. Dealing with them properly requires coordination and commitment across different units and agencies. Establishing those commitments, the consultants claimed, was "like pulling teeth."
- Management has failed to understand or support it. "We are left to push from down here. . . . it should not be up to us."
- Problem solving brings an unfamiliar degree of discretion, and uncertain degrees of authorization. Teams are not sure what they are allowed to propose, and whether they can really commit agency resources through their action plans. The persistent uncertainty brings projects to a standstill.
- Project teams are generally incapable of sticking to the imposed rigor of the approach. They don't understand why the different stages are necessary. "That puts enormous pressure on us [the facilitators], if we are the only ones interested in doing it right."
- Engaging external parties without offering them any kind of veto or vote over the action plan strikes participants as awkward. These terms of engagement are unfamiliar to all the participants.
- Problem solving is regarded by many as an alternative to enforcement, and is, consequently, written off as "one of the fashionable new soft options being pushed by senior management as they sell out to political pressures."

Such objections should be noted and must be taken seriously. They can all be dealt with, and have been dealt with by agencies that have persevered in constructing, formalizing, and institutionalizing problem-oriented capabilities. The majority of police departments, however, have not dealt with them, even in 2015. So it is worth pointing out some of the particular traps that the police profession has encountered and distortions that have appeared.

Reduced Form: Problem Solving as a Matter of Style for Beat Officers

One very early misunderstanding was to imagine that problem solving was only for beat officers, who might be expected to spot persistent problems at the beat level and learn how to deal with them intelligently and effectively. A problem-orientation thus became an issue of professional style for beat officers, and the problem-solving "guides" of the period were pocket-sized, designed to be carried around by beat officers on patrol.

Goldstein remarked on this early form, appreciating the localized successes it produced, but regretting the resulting inability to address larger or more widespread concerns: "But, too often, these commendable efforts [of individual police officers] are peripheral to everything else they do; sporadic; improvised; lacking in official support; and achieved despite the formal requirements of the bureaucracy."[23]

The appeal of this particular reduced form to executives is obvious: very little organizational support is needed (apart from some orientation and training for beat officers) and the department does not have to create any formal systems to manage problem-based work. This version does not place any serious demands on organizational resources and hardly requires managerial involvement. As Goldstein noted, this version can run at the ground level even while the department lacks any higher-level vision or structure for implementing the strategy.

One important probative question for departmental executives would be "is problem-solving for the beat officers or for the department?" If the strategy is for the department, then the department needs formal systems for identifying problems at multiple levels (including citywide), allocating personnel and financial resources, providing analytic support, managing collaborations with other agencies, vetting proposed action plans, monitoring impacts, and making decisions about when and why projects should be opened, closed, expanded, contracted, or redirected. In short, problem solving requires formal management and an executive-level commitment to driving, guiding, supporting, and managing a portfolio of problem-based projects. Problem solving cannot survive if it is merely an idea; it needs systems and protocols. It needs to be managed as seriously as every other kind of work the department does; otherwise, it can never compete and will not survive.

Reduced Form: Limiting Attention to Particular Dimensions

Harms come in a multitude of different shapes. In introducing the concept of problem-oriented policing for law enforcement, Herman Goldstein devoted considerable time and energy persuading the profession to use analytic methods beyond traditional "hot-spot" analyses. Pin-maps, showing crime locations, had long decorated precinct commanders' office walls. Clusters of pins represented hot spots, and hot spots showed police where to pay special attention. With the advent of computers, the pin-maps morphed into analytic software packages for "spatial and temporal analysis of crime." The medium was different, and the analytic methods more sophisticated, but the basic idea was the same.

Goldstein decried the narrowness of this one analytic approach.[24] He pointed out that not only did police tend to rely on one analytic approach; worse, they relied on one standard tactical response—termed directed patrol—whenever this analysis showed them a concentration. Directed patrol meant flooding the particular area at the relevant times with uniformed patrols to suppress the "crime problem."

Problems, for policing, come in many different shapes and sizes. Some problems are genuinely local, some citywide, and some (like major security and terrorism threats) national or international in scope. Some problems are geographic (and therefore susceptible to place-based or hot-spot analysis), but many are not. Recognizing the pervasiveness of the use of pin-maps as a form of crime analysis within the police profession, and recognizing that, with the advent of modern technology, spatial and temporal analysis remain the principal and pre-eminent form of analysis, Professor Herman Goldstein sought:

> To jolt the profession into a broader analytic versatility, pointing out that crime problems come in many different shapes and sizes, and geography and time represent only two of at least a dozen relevant dimensions. Some crime problems revolve around repeat offenders, even though the crime locations are dispersed. Other crime problems result from competition or conflict between rival criminal enterprises in the same business. Some patterns involve particularly vulnerable classes of victims (for example, single-manned convenience stores as targets for robberies), or repeat victims, or methods of attack, or specific behaviors (for example, glue-sniffing in the schools), or specific commodities (for example, Oxycontin-related pharmacy break-ins), or features of architectural design that create opportunities for crime, and so on.[25]

Many problems, therefore, come in awkward, in-between shapes and sizes that do not align neatly with existing organizational or jurisdictional boundaries. Effectiveness in problem solving demands organizational fluidity and a willingness to form partnerships across functional and geographic divisions. The underlying principle for effective problem-oriented action is clear: "Respect the natural shape and size of the harm itself. Fashion your response around its structure, rather than forcing the harm into your structure. Use a control structure which mirrors the structure of the harm itself."[26]

Even though the broad challenge of problem-oriented policing was laid out more than twenty years ago, the intervening years have seen a variety of more concrete operational methods proliferate. These systems—such as Zero-Tolerance policing, hot-spots policing, situational crime control, intelligence-led policing, and predictive policing—give police departments a recipe for action, a tangible way to proceed. At the same time, unfortunately, they threaten to narrow the police profession's vision of problem solving. Each concrete implementation, being particular in one or several regards, chips away at the versatility of the underlying notion.

Zero-Tolerance policing, or aggressive street-order maintenance, represents a default tactical approach. It is not only highly particular, but offensive to many communities and potentially corrosive of community trust. Hot-spots policing can only identify and focus on problems that have a specific and highly localized geographic concentration. Situational crime control focuses attention on a limited subset of precursor factors, namely those that have to do with environmental design and control of spaces.

Intelligence-led policing focuses heavily on dangerous and prolific offenders, and in some jurisdictions, it incorporates a focus on a short list of other problem types, as well. The focus on persistent and serious offenders is also narrow in its own way. Adopting an "offender-focus" serves departments well, of course, when they confront problems that do, in fact, stem from the conduct of a small number of egregious actors. For these problems, dealing with the few key offenders provides an efficient focus. But for any other kind of problem an offender-focus is not useful; it is neither the right way to think, nor to set priorities, nor to organize action.

Predictive policing, even though it is still too early to say exactly how this idea will evolve, seems likely to perpetuate a primary focus on geographic and temporal analysis, even if it refines and adds precision to that approach.

Reduced Form: Narrower Versions of CompStat

Implementations of CompStat have undoubtedly focused management attention on certain types of crime-reduction imperatives, and produced important results. In many departments, however, CompStat implementations have been treated as de facto substitutes for any broader problem-solving approach, thereby restricting or narrowing both the types of problems police can address and the range of solutions they are able to consider. The CompStat model, as it is generally understood, can be decidedly narrow in several of the ways in which problem solving is supposed to be broad. In its bare-bone versions, the CompStat model might be restrictive in any or all of the following ways. As discussed in detail in chapter 1, CompStat models may:

- Focus only on reported crime data (thus potentially neglecting the use of other data sources, and possibly short-changing problems not properly reflected in reported crime data).
- Focus solely on "reducing the numbers" (this could result in a lack of sensitivity to under-reported crimes, and introduce or exacerbate the dangers of recording biases and data distortions stemming from high-pressure use of numerical performance imperatives).

- Analyze crime patterns principally by precinct, and within precincts, with a heavy emphasis on geographic and temporal analysis (that is, potentially overlooking all the other dimensions in which crime patterns might naturally be defined).
- Automatically delegate responsibility for control to the precinct commanders (regardless of the size and shape of the problems to be addressed).
- Emphasize particular types of intervention (for example, focusing on aggressive order maintenance tactics for establishing police control over streets and public places).
- Employ distinctive managerial styles (for example, replicating the famously aggressive and adversarial tone with which the early CompStat meetings in New York City were conducted).

The particularity of such models is in tension with versatile and mature problem-solving approaches. Departments that rely too heavily on specific forms may end up forcing problems into the wrong mold and missing the opportunities for effective action that might materialize if only they could organize around the problems themselves rather than automatically trying to make the problems conform to predefined departmental modes of operation.

Problem solving works best when a department retains a task-focus, and organizes itself in ways that reflect the structure of the risks, harms, or problems in the field. Many departments get stuck in a tool-focus or a system-focus, so firmly committed to their own analytic and operational methods that they can no longer recognize when they are not appropriate. These reduced forms, implemented as governing organizational systems, become, in the minds of executives, "the way we do business, any business."

Table 3-1 provides a series of diagnostic study questions that police executives might consider if they want to challenge their organization on the maturity and versatility of its problem-solving capabilities and infrastructure. The table is based on a very simple definition of problem-solving success, namely, the ability "to spot emerging problems early and suppress them before they do much damage."[27] Table 3-1 recognizes the formidable challenge of turning that simple idea—spotting and suppressing emerging risks—into a form of professional competence for a sizable organization. To that end, the left-hand column unpacks an organizational problem solving or operational risk-management capability into six distinct elements.[28] The right-hand column then poses a number of diagnostic questions, relating to each of these six elements, that any management team can use to review its department's progress and identify any critical needs in terms of systems necessary to support a versatile problem-solving capability.

Inadequate Forms of Analytic and Research Support

The fourth major obstacle to the maturation of the problem-oriented approach is inadequate analytic support. This is the subject for the next chapter. Part of this problem is the simple lack of requisite analytic resources and skills within police departments. This deficiency was noted by Goldstein in 2003, and has not changed much since.[29]

Problem-oriented work is intensively analytical in its very nature. Problems have to be detected first, which may involve pattern-recognition and anomaly detection. Then they have to be studied, scoped, and circumscribed so that some reasonable sense can be developed of what the problem is, how widespread, in what ways is it concentrated, and how the problem works. Once the decision is made to launch a project, relevant metrics

TABLE 3-1. Elements of an Effective Problem-Solving System

Elements	Related diagnostic and study questions
1. Ability to identify crime patterns and other risk concentrations early in their life cycle, *before* they do much damage.	a. Where, within the department, does responsibility lie for spotting emerging problems? b. What methods are used for this task? c. Is the department better at spotting certain types of problems than others? d. Does the department have difficulty spotting problems of shapes and sizes that do not align naturally with existing organizational structures?
2. Commitment to scan proactively for *emergent and unfamiliar* risks, using a broad range of data sources and information-gathering techniques, and a set of exploratory and imaginative analytic and data-mining approaches sufficient to reveal issues never seen before, as well as the recurrence of familiar ones.	a. What data sources and analytic methods does the department use to identify developing patterns and trends early in their life cycle? b. Where does responsibility for this task lie? c. How much is the department biased toward familiar types of analysis (for examples, spatial and temporal hotspot analysis, division of crime rates by precinct, and so on) at the expense of a potentially broader range of methods? d. Is analytic support available to problem-solving teams on an ongoing basis, *after* the problem has been identified and a project launched?

Elements	Related diagnostic and study questions
3. Formal managerial system for reviewing problem nominations, prioritizing problems for attention, appointing project teams, and then managing and monitoring the department's portfolio of risk-mitigation/problem-solving projects.	a. Is this type of work centrally coordinated? b. Is it clear which managers or group of managers have responsibility for prioritizing and selecting problems for departmental attention? c. Have the criteria for problem selection been established, and are they generally known and understood? d. Does the department effectively track its portfolio of problem-based projects? e. Are mid-level managers familiar with the phases or stages of major problem-solving projects? f. Has the department developed formal systems for periodic review and oversight of problem-solving projects under way? g. What proportion of middle and upper managers have experience in conducting periodic *project review* meetings with project teams? h. Do the department's external reporting mechanisms formally incorporate project-based accomplishments?

TABLE 3-1. Elements of an Effective Problem-Solving System (Cont.)

Elements	Related diagnostic and study questions
4. Organizational fluidity to elevate risks identified to the appropriate level, so that the organization can gather relevant resources and attention around them, taking care to respect the natural size and dimensions of the problem, or risk concentration, itself.	a. What delegation options are available, within the department, for tackling problems of different shapes and size? b. At how many different *levels* within the department can problem-solving projects be organized and conducted? c. Do managers know how to organize projects that require the involvement of multiple units within the department but are not actually "department-wide"?
5. Willingness to engage in an open-minded search for tailor-made solutions, sufficient to mitigate each identified risk to acceptable levels, and in a resource-efficient manner.	a. How broad is the range of solutions actually deployed in response to identified problems? b. To what extent is the solution set biased toward traditional methods (for example, directed patrol, street-level order-maintenance tactics, and so forth)?
6. System for organizational *learning*, so that those engaged in problem solving can access knowledge accumulated by others.	c. What form does this system take, and where is it located? d. How "rich" is the information contained within it? e. What proportion of the department's personnel have ever accessed it?

must be established by which progress could be measured. Those project-specific metrics ought to be benchmarked before any action steps are taken; otherwise, nobody will ever know if the interventions succeed. During action stages, the relevant metrics need to be monitored so that progress can be evaluated. At some point determinations have to be made about whether the problem is significantly abated, and abated enough to justify closing the project so the organization can move on to the next problem. Every stage of the problem-solving process requires analytic support, and (based on experience across a broad range of other risk-control domains) my rule of thumb is that 20 percent of the effort that goes into a properly run problem-solving project will be analytical in nature.

The analytic methods that are available within police departments tend to be oriented around the particular operational methods that have been adopted. If the operational methods focus on one dimension (like space, or repeat offenders), then the accompanying analytic methods will be particular and made to match. Notice how systems such as CompStat and intelligence-led policing represent methods for defining and dividing crime-control work; they each have their own relevant analytic methods. The uses of data and the forms of analysis that each approach recognizes serve to reinforce the particular operational approach. CompStat first divides up any available crime data by precinct, because the CompStat process subsequently divides and allocates the responsibility for action by precinct. Similarly, intelligence-led policing does the analysis by offender (or offender-group), because intelligence-led policing subsequently sets the agenda and prioritizes the department's attention by ranking and targeting offenders and offender groups.

Notice the circularity trap. The department has selected certain operational methods. It then commissions the analyses that will detect the problems of the right shape and size to fit those operational methods. Any analysis conducted, therefore, will find the problems with the right dimensionality, and discovery of them will act to confirm to the organization that the choice of operational methods is appropriate. Meanwhile, risk concentrations of different shapes (that is, those defined in different dimensions) are unlikely to be noticed, and, thus, less likely to be addressed. A CompStat-style analysis is less likely to reveal problems that straddle precincts or are citywide. Analysis supporting intelligence-led policing probably would not pick up a concentration of domestic violence committed around public holidays or around major sporting events, because the analysis is not oriented around those dimensions.

Given the existence of this circularity trap, it is interesting to see what police officials make of crime problems that—in terms of size and shape—do not align either with their analytic traditions or with the organizational machinery available to them. Two behaviors seem all too common in practice. Officials confronted with awkwardly shaped problems will be tempted, either to:

- Carve the problem into pieces, so that the pieces *do* fit their existing machinery (but this leads to inefficiencies, as no one is then in a position to address the issue in a suitably holistic way or to design a coherent and integrated response)
- Assume that, if the problem doesn't fit their system, then controlling it cannot possibly be their responsibility (if it is not about a repeat offender, then the intelligence-led policing unit is surely not responsible; if the problem does not produce a visible concentration of reported crime within one precinct, then who—under CompStat—will take responsibility for it?)

The only way to break out of this circularity trap—where operational methods determine what analyses are commissioned, and the analyses conducted determine the types of problems that are detected—is to throw wide open the analytic operation and demand much greater versatility. The cycle has to be broken at the *analytic* end. Data of many different types must be sliced and diced in a multitude of different ways, regardless of whether the organization is poised to respond to the unfamiliar and awkwardly shaped issues that might surface. By deliberately increasing the versatility of the analytic operation, the organization increases the range of problems it can detect. Discovering new types of problems, in turn, then challenges the organization to develop relevant and novel operational responses.

The other substantial piece of this analytic puzzle involves the nature of collaboration between scholars and practitioners. Such collaboration is increasingly energetic and well funded, and surely brings benefits to both parties: practitioners gain access to sophisticated research methods, and academics get something practical and important to work on.

But the dominant form of the interactions between practitioners and scholars that now occur—which are heavily focused on social science methods, program evaluation, and evidence-based policing—are not exactly what is needed to support problem-oriented policing. Federal grant funding, which is also heavily oriented toward evaluations, has served to reinforce the centrality of social science methods in supporting the profession.

Of course, there's nothing wrong with social science methods being available to the police profession; there is, indeed, a valuable role to be played by academia in helping to evaluate police programs. The trouble is that this is not the brand of analytic support that problem-oriented policing really needs!

In specifying the nature of requisite analytic support for policing, neither the demand side (police practitioners) nor the supply side (academic researchers) seems to be able to articulate the nature of the current misalignment, or to say what should be done to correct it.

Hopefully, the following chapter will shed some light on this puzzle, helping to specify what kinds of scientific support policing needs and how to broaden the forms of research and analysis available. In particular, it questions the relative importance of the inquiry methods of the social sciences when contrasted with those of the natural sciences. Social scientists tend to inquire, "Which programs work?" Natural scientists tend to inquire, "How does the world work?" These different instincts lead to quite different kinds of investigation. The following chapter argues that, to provide the analytic support that problem-oriented policing requires, natural science inquiry methods are essential; and it is these methods that have, to date, been seriously neglected.

FOUR

Governing Science

A favorite family pastime is to discover road signs that, either through ambiguous wording or lack of punctuation, lend themselves to multiple different interpretations. One of my daughter's favorites has always been:

If read as presumably intended, the sign warns motorists there might be children nearby, and SLOW is a command. But my daughter points out that SLOW could be an adjective, instead. Perhaps motorists should allow more time for the (slower) children to get out of the way. And, she says, if this appeared outside the headmaster's office rather than by the side of the road, it might be a reminder to the children themselves to conduct themselves with decorum and not go tearing around.

Likewise, the title of this chapter, "Governing Science," could suggest three different meanings in the context of policing. Perhaps the word *governing* is an adjective, in which case it would be the science that is doing the governing. Then the object might be to explore and define the science that should govern police as they consider how to conduct their business.

A second interpretation could be that governing science is a job to be done, with perhaps a hint that science (or scientists) might need to be controlled or restrained. In the context of policing, a discussion along these lines might set appropriate limits for the role of science and the influence of scientists.

A third possible interpretation arises from reading the phrase *governing science* the same way we read the phrases *fishing tackle* and *climbing gear.* There is a challenge to be met: to catch fish, or to conquer mountains, or to provide quality, democratic governance. Through years of accumulated experience and often-painful experimentation, those facing the challenge develop a sense of needs. To meet those needs, they invent or design various types of tackle (for fishing), gear (for climbing), or science (for governing) to help get the job done. If we wanted to know what the science for governing was that might improve the quality of life in a democracy, we would first focus on clarifying the role for police within the broader frame of democratic governance (that was the work of chapter 2); and then we could define the types of science and areas of application that might best serve in support of that mission.

The merits of close collaboration between the fields of policing and scholarship are obvious. Anyone who cares about policing cherishes that collaboration enormously. It has already delivered considerable benefits for policing and is poised to deliver many more. Everyone should want that relationship to flourish. However, at this time, the relationship remains fragile, and much harm might be done if we accept a vision for the future of the relationship that is somehow misguided, inappropriate, or off base.

The Evidence-Based Policing Movement

The evidence-based policing movement (EBP) espouses a very particular vision of how the relationship between scholars and police should work. This chapter examines the underlying assumptions of that broader EBP movement, as what EBP proposes requires some counterbalance and caution, particularly at this time in the development of policing and as we consider the forms of analysis required to support problem-oriented policing.

Evidence-based policing rests on an underlying assumption that the only way for police to know what works is for them to allow social scientists—the professional evaluators—to make determinations for them, and that social scientists, being trained in statistical and empirical methods (whereas police generally are not) can offer their "high science" of controlled experiments and sophisticated program evaluation methods. Police ought, then, to be keenly interested in and grateful for the truths that social science methods make available.

Furthermore, the champions of EBP propose that police should subsequently limit themselves to using only those programs that the scholarly community has been able to establish as effective. In other words, science should govern policing. Thus, the central message in the EBP movement aligns quite well with the first of the three possible interpretations of *governing science.*

Lawrence Sherman, describing the underlying theory of EBP in 1998, proposes: "One way to describe people who try to apply research is the role of 'evidence cop.' More like a traffic cop than Victor Hugo's detective Javert, the evidence cop's job is to redirect practice through compliance rather than punishment. While this job may be as challenging as herding cats, it still consists of pointing professionals to practice 'this way, not that way.'"[1]

Police practitioners might bristle at the notion of being herded (like cats) by social scientists. However, Sherman pushes further, proposing that police be evaluated on the basis of whether they conform to what the researchers have recommended:

> Evidence-based policing is the use of the best available research on the outcomes of police work to implement guidelines and evaluate agencies, units, and officers. Put more simply, evidence-based policing uses research to guide practice and evaluate practitioners. . . . Evidence-based policing is about two very different kinds of research: basic research on what works best . . . and ongoing outcomes research about the results each unit is actually achieving by applying (or ignoring) basic research in practice.[2]

This kind of language infuriates police practitioners. Should police managers—who carry all of the responsibility for day-to-day policing and suffer directly the consequences of failure—be chastised by social scientists (who carry none of the responsibility) simply because they chose to ignore a published research finding or executed an untested or unproven strategy? The idea that science should guide and govern policing in such a way—so that scientists discipline practitioners who don't comply with scientific guidelines—seems ridiculous to practitioners and completely inappropriate to many academics as well. But exactly *why* the relationship should *not* be structured this way is a serious enough question, which this chapter seeks to answer.

Many of us are more attracted to the third interpretation of *governing science* that first develops a vision of policing in a democracy, and then defines the science required to support it. This vision emphasizes multiple dimensions of performance and value, and embraces a range of operational styles that move considerably beyond the replication of a small number of "proven" or approved programs. This third interpretation also seems most neutral on the question of which partner (police or science) is supposed to govern the other. It suggests a more healthy collaboration in the long term, with each party delivering its appropriate and respective contributions in support of democratic policing.

Given the more aggressive claims of some of EBP's champions, some serious work remains to be done along the lines of the second interpretation. Police themselves need to do some governing. The police profession needs:

- A more comprehensive view of the range of scientific methods relevant to policing.
- A proper understanding of where different types of science belong.
- Confidence to specify the investments in science that they most need.
- A clear sense of what might be at risk when scholars claim too much or stray beyond their proper role.

Periodic Reminders for Social Scientists

Social scientific research methods have their place, of course, in adding to knowledge. The evidence-based policy movement in general emphasizes program evaluation techniques and concentrates on determining causation. Many of the relevant research techniques require analytical sophistication. Valid experiments take considerable care and skill to design, conduct, and evaluate. The tools of EBP are expensive, but anyone who values knowledge should surely value methods that can help produce it. Reliable findings about what works, and what doesn't, can help avoid the perpetuation of useless practices and can prevent police officials or politicians from making bogus claims about their achievements or perpetuating useless programs for personal or political reasons. Police managers should surely take note of experimental results and research findings that impinge on operational decisions they need to make. Not to do so would be professionally irresponsible.

From time to time, though, it seems that social scientists need to be reminded of a few things:

- They have no monopoly on useful knowledge or on useful methods for acquiring it.
- Experience and skills count, too; there are myriad ways of discovering useful truths without the elaborate machinery of social science evaluations.
- The majority of scientific advances benefiting humankind have arisen and become firmly established without their help.
- "Lay inquiry," with its messier methods and iterative ad hoc experimentation, contributes mightily to the development of knowledge.
- Program evaluation comes very late in a long process of research, problem identification, diagnosis, and policy development. All the earlier stages—spotting problems in the first place, scoping them, figuring out their structure and dynamics, and designing a set of plausibly effective interventions—require analytic support, too, but not normally of the specific types offered by the conventions of social science research.

In 1990, Charles Lindblom, a professor of political science at Yale University, published *Inquiry and Change: The Troubled Attempt to Understand and Shape Society*. Lindblom set out to examine "how people in contemporary industrialized societies, competently or not, go about gathering and analyzing information in grappling with social problems."[3] Lindblom's "people" (who go about this task) include politicians, citizens, natural scientists, social scientists, practitioners, and ordinary but curious folk, whom he labels "lay inquirers." By no means did Lindblom set out to attack the social sciences, but in the process of evaluating relative contributions from different types of inquiry and groups of inquirers, he does end up giving social scientists a very hard time. They make the mistake, he says, of overvaluing their own highly technical approaches to the acquisition of knowledge and of presuming that opinions reached any other way must stem from unfounded beliefs or foolishness:

> To be sure, many social scientists and other commentators on social problem solving have fallen into believing that decision makers can approach problems in only one of two ways: either technically, as means to ends, or with all the rigidities, obfuscations, and imprecisions of ideology. But a third option is available: selective and varied probing of both ends and means, as well as of other values.[4]

Mark Moore also comments on the challenge that a continuum of knowledge poses, and the perils of ignoring everything between the extremes:

> Both the research and the practice field in policing face the important question of how far down the path of scientific sophistication they should go in their combined efforts to establish a firm experiential and empirical basis for policing. More provocatively put, they have to decide what to do with the knowledge that lies between mere opinion on one hand, and results established through randomized trials on the other.[5]

A 1995 paper by Moore examines the linkages between knowledge and policy formulation, specifically in the context of community policing and violence prevention in the United States.[6] Moore recognizes, of course, the value of social science research methods and acknowledges their place in policy development, but, like Lindblom, he warns against giving them too central a role in policy development:

> Let me hasten to say that I don't think that social scientists are wrong to want knowledge to guide policy. Indeed, it would be irresponsible *not* to use thought, evidence, and experience to guide policymakers when they commit substantial public resources to a particular goal. Instead, I think their mistake lies in having too narrow a view of what constitutes knowledge valuable enough to use in confronting public problems, too rigid an idea about where and how useful knowledge accumulates in the society, and too unrealistic a view of how knowledge might best be diffused and deployed in aid of both immediate action and continued learning.[7]

Not Just Another Periodic Reminder

My purpose here is not just to issue yet another periodic reminder. Others have done that job quite thoroughly elsewhere and continue to do it in a variety of fields, whenever social scientists exaggerate their own contributions or attempt to exert control over practitioners (that is, to govern policymaking). The contention of this chapter is stronger, more particular, and timely, I hope. I believe that we are in a particularly important period in the development of police science, requiring enriched and productive relationships between police and academia. I also believe that much harm might result if we give EBP a dominant position in the context of that relationship.

Why Police Should Govern the Role of Science

There are three reasons why the police profession should work particularly hard to govern science at this time.

Incompatibility

The methods championed by proponents of EBP are fundamentally incompatible with the operational realities of problem-oriented policing. Although many departments have made some progress in learning some particular forms of the problem-solving method, relatively few have developed the kind of versatility that Herman Goldstein originally envisaged. Fewer still have developed the range of analytic techniques, organizational fluidity, and related managerial skills that would enable them to work effectively on problems of all shapes and sizes. The maturing of the problem-solving approach remains a priority for the profession, particularly as the range of threats confronted by police expands beyond those that are neighborhood or place-based. EBP represents a potential threat to, and a diversion from, the styles of scientific inquiry needed to advance the art of problem-oriented policing. Social scientists championing the cause of EBP, if given their head at this particular point in time, could unwittingly obstruct the maturation of the problem-solving strategy.

Methodology

The social-scientific research methods embraced by EBP represent a tiny fraction of the scientific methods relevant to policing. They should, therefore, represent a small portion of the relevant investment portfolio, and should garner a relatively small fraction of the attention given to science. Giving too much attention

to EBP at this time necessarily means giving too little attention to a much broader range of scientific inquiry methods that
deserve higher priority. Equating EBP with science is grossly
misleading.

Relationship Form

The form of the relationship between police and academia
envisaged by EBP is unstable and unsustainable. There is too
much in it for the social scientists and almost nothing in it for
the police. That is precisely why the champions of EBP press
so hard, and why police continue to show so little interest and
remain largely unaffected. The relationship needs to be rede-
fined. The prescription is wrong. If EBP is given a central place
in the relationship, the relationship may, in fact, be damaged,
and many other opportunities for productive collaboration may
be lost as a result.

The following sections examine these three arguments in
more detail.

Fundamental Incompatibility with Problem-Oriented Policing

EBP is incompatible with POP for the following seven reasons.

Too Slow

EBP is too slow in making determinations to support operational problem solving. The problems that spawned the interventions have themselves long since passed, or morphed into
another form, by the time the interventions can pass through the
elaborate experimental and evaluative procedures espoused by

EBP. EBP may eventually produce dependable results with high levels of confidence, but these typically arrive between three and five years after the development of an intervention. This makes EBP findings relevant to operations only when it evaluates programs that are permanent or long-standing and change very little over time or across jurisdictions. Such programs are not the focus of problem-oriented policing, which seeks ad hoc and sufficient solutions for the problems of the day and then moves on quickly to the problems of tomorrow, expecting that those will be different.

No New Solutions

EBP produces no new solutions and may even *narrow* the range of solutions available. Proponents of EBP suggest or imply that police should only use those methods that EBP scholars have already been able to validate. Problem-oriented policing, by contrast, encourages creativity and rapid experimentation, thus dramatically *expanding* the range of techniques and methods available. Ceding too much influence to EBP may, therefore, produce a bias against action and too narrow a search for solutions.[8]

Wrong Level of Focus

Social scientists focus on subtle effects at high (aggregate) levels; problem solving focuses on much more obvious effects but at lower levels. Social scientists (and economists) have tended to conduct macro-level analyses on aggregate data sets. They like to use sophisticated statistical methods on large data sets to reveal subtle correlations and causations between factors and outcomes. Inheriting these tendencies, EBP emphasizes the importance of evaluating the effect that particular programs (for example, DARE, early childhood intervention programs, or random patrols) might or might not have on overall crime rates or on some major category of crime rates (for example, violence), delinquency rates, or addiction rates later in life.

Problem solving, as taught by Goldstein, emphasizes careful disaggregation of broad crime categories, following the intuition that major crime problems have many parts (lower-level components) and that, usually, the various parts each behave differently and depend on different factors. Once the lower-level objects have been found (often through analysis), then each one can be studied and "unpicked." In *The Character of Harms*, I have described how the art of navigating these lower-level strata of problems or harms is emerging as a vital professional skill for regulators and law enforcement:

> The habits of mind . . . have something in common with the skills involved in a relatively mundane task: the undoing of knots. Give a knotted mass of string to an adult, who has developed all of the relevant cognitive skills (and maybe had some experience, too), and watch how they behave. Notice how they hold the whole object up to the light, and look at it this way, then that way, turning it around and around, examining it diligently from all sides—careful all the time not to pull or tug or to make matters worse—until they begin to understand the structure of the thing itself. As the structure of the knot becomes clearer, so the components or stages of a plan begin to form in their minds. . . . If they understood the structure correctly, and fashioned a plan accordingly, the knot eventually falls apart, and is no more.
>
> In the regulatory field, we have a growing list of harms undone, knots untied, risk-concentrations eliminated or substantially mitigated. Invariably, the knots undone by regulators, or others who act in this vein, are not broad, general phenomena (at the level of "air pollution," or "corruption,"

or "motor vehicle accidents"). Nor are they minutiae, representing single incidents (of crime, or injury, or death). These knots untied, these harms undone, all lie *in between,* where the object of study is larger than a single incident or event, but smaller than a general class of harms. It is in this *in-between* realm where much exciting work seems to take place, amid the complex and multi-layered texture that connects individual incidents at the bottom to entire classes of risk (with their one- or two-word descriptions) at the top.[9]

The impetus for problem-oriented policing arises in part from the realization that it makes little sense to focus on general programmatic treatments for general crime categories if the texture beneath is, in fact, highly complex, variegated, and populated by many unlike objects. Problem-oriented policing is born from a conviction that working in the textured layers beneath (rather than at the level of generalities or major crime categories) offers greater promise and quicker results.

Reduced Experimentation

Ironically, greater influence for EBP may reduce the rate of experimentation in policing. Professional researchers, as masters of experimental design and evaluation, regard themselves as the authority on what constitutes a "proper" experiment. Thus, police agencies where the evidence cops hold sway might be less inclined to proceed with any experimentation that falls short of scholarly standards. In particular, such agencies might be less inclined to proceed with the type of iterative, developmental, and exploratory experimentation that characterizes problem solving.

EBP proponents want valid controls as well as crystal-clear specification of the intervention being tested. Their design purpose is to establish causal connections. However, problem solvers' purposes and methods are different. They seek to quickly generate creative, plausibly effective solutions, which are worth trying just because there is a chance they might fix the problem.[10] Problem solvers certainly want to see problems reduced or eliminated and should be methodologically rigorous when it comes to monitoring the abatement of the specific problems addressed so they can tell when progress is being made (hence, Goldstein's strong emphasis on measurement and monitoring).[11] However, they are not so concerned about proving causality. Consequently, problem solving does not normally impose the additional methodological constraints that would support determinations of causality. Problem solvers use iterative techniques, short-cycle development, and rapid, early assessments of impact, followed by ad hoc and multiple adjustments—all of which confound the technical methods of social science evaluation. As John Eck has pointed out, "Rigorous evaluations are an awkward, inefficient, and unnatural way to learn about what works when we are interested in small-scale, small-claim, discrete interventions."[12] Hence the danger: if EBP is allowed to set the standards for police experimentation, then much valuable experimentation might be curtailed.

Perpetuation of Old Mind-Sets

EBP may reinforce and perpetuate the program-centric mindset in policing, which problem-oriented policing was supposed to dispel. The entire motivation for problem solving—not just in policing but also across the whole field of social regulation—is to help public agencies understand the deficiencies of a functional or programmatic view of their work, and discover what it means to be task-based rather than tool-based.[13] Skilled craftsmen do not spend the day staring at the array of tools hanging from the workshop wall, contemplating which ones work and which ones don't; rather, the craftsman stands at the task bench and focuses on what must be accomplished. Problem solving represents a fundamental departure from a tool-centric or program-centric approach, because it recreates the experience of the craftsman in his shop, standing at the task bench, studying the task, facing the dawning and uncomfortable realization that "I don't have a tool for this," at which point the successful craftsman invents and fabricates a new tool tailor-made for the job.

Proponents of EBP argue that they, too, realize that programs should not be mindlessly copied from one jurisdiction to another. They acknowledge the need to anticipate adjustments and refinements based on local conditions when replicating successful programs. However, this is a tiny move and not enough to restore the appropriate frame of mind for problem solving. Make some minor adjustments to a hammer and it is still fundamentally a hammer. Adjust your saw blade, and it still only makes cuts. A tool-focus is what we were trying to escape. An adjustable wrench is still a wrench, and no amount of fiddling with it will help if the task is to retrieve a loose screw lodged deep in an engine crankcase, and the craftsman has no suitable tool for that. Making tools adjustable might make them more broadly useful. Nevertheless, focusing first on programs is still a fundamentally different frame of mind than focusing first on problems; these two mind-sets lead to entirely different organizational behaviors and responses.

Not Supportive of Best Options

With its reliance on statistical techniques, EBP may not recognize or reward the best problem-solving performance. In any risk-control or harm-reduction setting real success means "spotting emerging problems early and suppressing them before they do much damage."[14] Sophisticated analysis and pattern recognition capabilities, along with bristling intelligence antennae and other forms of alertness and vigilance, can help an agency spot emerging problems earlier rather than later. The earlier the spotting, the less noticeable (in a statistical sense) will be the suppressing. The problem itself and the effects of any intervention will each be less discernible through quantitative analysis if the action was early and swift. By contrast, problems that have been allowed to grow hopelessly out of control, and which are then dramatically reduced through some sizable effort, are much more likely to show up as demonstrable successes through the evaluative lenses of EBP. EBP's methods will mostly recognize only bigger, later suppressions and may not be able to discern or appreciate the deftness and nimbleness that constitutes real problem-solving success. Allowing EBP to arbitrate what works could have the perverse effect of leading the profession to celebrate only those crime-reduction successes that had been preceded by substantial failures.

Intervention-Focused

EBP focuses only on specific interventions and pays little attention to the development of an agency's problem-solving capacity and skills. Problem-oriented policing has profound implications for almost every aspect of a police department's operations:

- It requires new sets of skills for officers engaging in it.
- It requires extensive analytic support at several different stages of the problem-solving process.
- It makes senior officers responsible for tackling a portfolio of problems or risks rather than managing a portfolio of programs or functions.

- It severely stretches the internal fabric of an agency because the majority of problems simply don't fit neatly within existing organizational units.
- It plunges the agency into a constellation of complicated inter-agency and cross-sectoral partnerships, simply because real-world problems don't respect agency boundaries either.

EBP focuses closely on the evaluation of specific interventions and very little, if at all, on the development of agency competencies. Even interventions that failed—in the narrow sense of having produced no measurable impact on levels of crime or disorder—may nevertheless have contributed to agency experience, developed the capacity and confidence of its officers, enriched important partnerships with other parts of government, and strengthened community engagement through collaborative efforts. For problem-oriented policing to mature, the profession must pay significant attention to all of these other forms of progress, which EBP tends to overlook.

EBP Fights Back

Several of these arguments have been made before, and some of the more enlightened advocates for EBP seem prepared to acknowledge many or all of them. But the EBP movement seems unwilling to let problem-oriented policing alone or to recognize it as an area where EBP's preferred methods might have severely limited value. Curiously, as if problem-solving represents some kind of threat to the status of social science, EBP seeks to reassert control, and its supporters appear to have pursued two particular strategies for this purpose.

Evaluating Problem-Oriented Policing as a General Strategy

The first involves moving to a higher level. EBP may concede that social science research methods cannot keep pace with operational policing, and might be too expensive and elaborate to apply to low-level and short-term problem-solving efforts, but they can surely evaluate the overall strategy of problem-solving! This represents an attractive proposition for the scholars, if only it were possible. They might be able to establish that problem-solving actually works to reduce crime and disorder, in which case EBP could share the credit for anything that problem-solving subsequently accomplished. Alternatively, perhaps scientific research might demonstrate conclusively that problem-oriented policing doesn't work at all, in which case all of the threats to the scientists' right to govern policing, laid out earlier, would simply fizzle away.

As a theoretical matter, evaluating an overall strategy (such as problem-oriented policing, for example) is quite different from evaluating a set of particular interventions that the strategy has produced.[15] As a practical matter, there is no way that the efficacy of problem-oriented policing, as an overall strategy, could be determined through formally structured experiments or evaluations. There are simply too many different forms of it, many of them deemed "shallow" one way or another by the scholars,[16] and too little maturity in terms of the broader versatility originally envisaged. The prospect of finding even fifty departments who operate the same version of problem-solving, and another fifty who clearly do not (for the sake of providing a suitable control group) seems extremely remote.

A recent study led by David Weisburd illustrates the difficulties involved in trying to evaluate problem-oriented policing as an overall strategy. It also provides a wonderful illustration of the consequences of focusing first on quality of evidence rather than on a broader search for operational insights. Four researchers set out to conduct a Campbell Systematic Review of existing literature to determine "whether POP is effective in reducing crime and disorder."[17] Following protocols established by the Campbell Collaboration,[18] these researchers first conducted a massive troll of the research literature, uncovering no fewer than 5,500 relevant articles and reports. They applied the standard methodological threshold tests and concluded that only ten of these studies (those that involved randomized or well-matched comparison groups) made the cut.

Weisburd and his fellow researchers then combined the findings from these ten studies, using meta-analysis techniques, and arrived at the conclusion that POP seemed to have some modest but, nevertheless, perceptible effect.[19] However, the researchers noted that, if they had chosen to use a different method of combining the results from these ten studies (a method called *vote counting*[20]), then the conclusion would have been entirely different (that is, "no discernible effect").[21] After all that effort, their eventual determination of whether POP has any effect at all hinges on the researchers' choice among available methods for combining the results.

There was potentially more encouraging news from the second part of this study. The authors noted that, by relaxing their methodological standards somewhat (admitting studies that had pre/post data but lacked control or comparison groups), they could bring in a further forty-five studies from the remaining pool. The combined results from this broader collection were "overwhelmingly in favor of POP effectiveness."[22] However, the authors then noted that combining the effects from a broad collection of problem-solving interventions, each aimed at quite different types of problems, seemed problematic. Indeed, it does. After all, the idea was to test the overall strategy of problem-oriented policing, not to try to combine a set of miscellaneous but particular interventions that problem-oriented approaches had produced. Using statistical aggregation techniques to combine outcomes from interventions focused on quite different types of problems seems vaguely bizarre. It is like posing some general and high-level question such as "Do drugs work?" and then trying to answer that question by combining studies involving quite different drugs, applied to patients with quite different conditions. Normally meta-analysis techniques are used to combine results from several implementations of the same program. Cognizant of this difficulty, Weisburd and colleagues add an appropriately cautious rider to these (initially more encouraging) results: "This diversity of programs and approaches also should bring caution to any conclusions drawn from our study."[23]

The net result? A mammoth undertaking, involving the review of 5,500 articles and reports, rejection of all but a handful of them because the evidence they contained was deemed not of sufficient quality, and sophisticated meta-analysis of the few that did clear the threshold, yielding highly tenuous conclusions that readers are advised to treat with "caution." For professional social scientists, this is a veritable tour de force, demonstrating the highest levels of technical and methodological sophistication. And for operational policing? Probably nothing much useful: no new insights or ideas, and no reliable conclusions. No wonder scholars across many policy domains are now asking, "What is it about experimental evaluation, or . . . quasi-experimental evaluation, which leads even the very best of it to yield so little?"[24]

Of course, had this review uncovered hundreds or thousands of properly conducted experiments, rather than only ten, then the results might have been more conclusive. Weisburd and his colleagues are quick to observe the general absence of such studies, concluding that "the evidence base in this area is deficient given the strong investment in POP."[25] How should we remedy that deficiency? Weisburd and colleagues offer the standard

EBP proposal that "a much larger number of studies is needed to draw strong generalizations regarding the possible effectiveness of POP."[26]

There might be some other ways to remedy the situation. One might pay more attention to other forms of evidence or ponder, at least for a moment, the insights and wisdom contained in the other 5,445 reports.

Gilles Paquet, former president of the Royal Society of Canada, describes a variety of "blockages" to the production of knowledge suitable for informing public policy and aims squarely at the evidence-based policy movement generally: "The second family of blockages pertains to the notion of evidence. It stems from a tendency of the fundamentalists to summarily reject a whole range of types of knowledge as irrelevant, if not meaningless, if that knowledge does not originate from the credentialized tribe and is not the result of work done according to certain prescribed protocols."[27]

Proponents of EBP have set the bar for *knowing* so high, and made the means for generating knowledge so particular, that they end up knowing relatively little. Operational police need to know much more, just well enough and much sooner, to keep up with the pace and variety of the challenges they face.

Focusing on Place-Based Problem-Solving Interventions

EBP will probably never manage to produce a convincing evaluation of problem-oriented policing at the level of a departmental strategy. Perhaps recognizing this, the EBP movement makes a second attempt to re-insert itself firmly into the problem-solving arena. If the research scientists can't keep pace with individual problem-solving projects and they have little hope of evaluating the overall strategy, then maybe they can find some particular version of problem-solving that can act as a proxy for the overall strategy and which they can actually evaluate. EBP does seem to have found one: the use of place-based interventions. Much of the current energy in the EBP movement seems to be gravitating to this area—testing the effects of order maintenance and other localized interventions—and confirming for us what must have seemed intuitively obvious to police executives for decades: place-based problems tend to have place-based solutions.

It seems somewhat curious that EBP, in trying to offer some insight on the efficacy of problem-oriented policing, would end up focusing on such an old and familiar police tradition, one that actually predates Goldstein. Perhaps EBP focuses on place-based interventions because place-based experiments are relatively easy to design and conduct. The data required to identify spatial (or temporal) concentrations already exist. The analysis required to identify geographic clusters is straightforward and familiar. Furthermore, places, when divided into treatment and control groups, don't complain, call their lawyers, or lodge constitutional objections about unequal treatment.[28]

Organizing experiments around other dimensions may be more difficult. Substantial ethical difficulties arise and potential legal challenges may result whenever randomized controlled experiments are organized around pervasively criminal families, classes of victims, or different cohorts of schoolchildren drawn into gang-related activity—where substantial groups of people end up getting quite different treatments.

"But, in medicine, they do that all the time," some may object. "They conduct experiments on issues of life and death, with human control groups, all day and every day." True. However, medical experimentation is based on informed consent and voluntary participation, features of the experimental environment that policing seldom enjoys.

One of the broader and more sophisticated inquiries into the efficacy of problem solving was conducted recently by Anthony Braga and Brenda Bond, working with the Lowell, Massachusetts, police department.[29] Through analysis, they identified thirty-four crime hot spots in Lowell and allocated seventeen of them to a treatment group and seventeen to a control group, using a matching procedure. Three types of problem-solving interventions were applied within the treatment group: (1) sustained programs of misdemeanor arrests, (2) other "situational" (that is, place-based) strategies, and (3) some "social service" strategies (referrals and other services offered to specific individuals).

Braga and Bond's analysis of the experiment, which employed mediation analysis and other highly sophisticated statistical methods, enabled them to draw two main conclusions: (1) a collection of interventions, "focused at specific high-activity crime and disorder places in the city," can generate crime prevention gains;[30] and (2) "the strongest crime prevention benefits were driven by situational strategies that attempted to modify the criminal opportunity structure at crime and disorder hot spot locations," with misdemeanor arrest strategies and social service–type interventions scoring less well.[31]

Should we, therefore, conclude that situational crime prevention techniques are hereby validated and that the alternate (people-based) strategies should continue to be regarded with continuing skepticism? I think not. I have complete confidence in these two authors' analytic skills and experimental disciplines, and the diligent cooperation of the Lowell Police Department under their chief at the time, Ed Davis. However, I have a strong suspicion that the conclusions the researchers could draw as a result of this experiment are not surprising and are largely determined by the way the experiment was designed. The crime concentrations selected as the foundation for the experiment were spatial. Experience with problem solving in a broad range of other domains teaches us that the dimensions in which a problem or risk is concentrated are often (but not always) closely related to the dimensionality of the solutions.[32] Place-based problems are more likely to have place-based remedies. Family-centered problems are more likely to respond to family-centric interventions. Social needs-based problems are more likely to benefit from the provision of social services. Thus, it is not fair to compare three classes of intervention, each organized around different dimensions, starting with only place-based crime concentrations. One might expect, or might even predict, that place-based strategies would come out on top.

It may be that criminologists conduct place-based experiments simply because they can. (In Weisburd and colleagues' Campbell Systematic Review, they found only four randomized studies among the 5,500 POP-related articles, and all four involved place-based experiments.) [33] Researchers may, therefore, be quicker to confirm the efficacy of place-based strategies than other types of problem-based interventions. The danger, of course, is that the audience for these evaluations might imagine this actually teaches us about what works and what doesn't in policing. What EBP can actually "prove" has as much to do with the limitations and feasibility of its own research methods as it has to do with what actually works. Perhaps this is why the list of approved interventions remains so short. The shortness of the list might have much less to do with the effectiveness of policing strategies and much more to do with the limitations of EBP's approved methodologies and the difficulties of applying them in the policing environment.

A Broader Range of Scientific Methods

The social sciences have an older brother, the natural sciences, with a better-established and more robust record of accomplishment. Natural scientists not only look into different areas (physics, biology, chemistry, astronomy, engineering) but also tend to inquire in different ways.

Social science experimental techniques tend to treat complex systems (for example, communities, families, school populations, and even crime organizations) as black boxes. Researchers can control the inputs, testing them in various combinations; and they can monitor what comes out at the other end of the box some time later (for example, delinquency rates, crime rates, addiction rates, or propensity for violence). They can then apply sophisticated statistical techniques to their accumulated data about inputs and outcomes, and draw causal inferences in some cases.

Natural scientists tend to have different instincts. They lift up the lid of the box and peer inside. They poke and prod around, not knowing at the outset what they expect to find, open to all sorts of possibilities, not yet knowing what tools they will need to probe further. Their inquiry methods are reflexive, which means that, as Gilles Paquet explains, "knowledge acquired gets integrated during the process; it influences the design and thereby modifies the outcome."[34] They do not emphasize any particular or preferred tool kit, nor do they have ingrained in their consciousness any formally approved hierarchy of evidence. They explore. They inspect mechanisms up close, rather than observing inputs and outcomes in the aggregate and from a distance. As Pawson and Tilley observed, very few experiments in natural science use experimental/control-group logic.[35]

Different Scientific Traditions

I remember a recent day-long meeting at Harvard University's School of Law that drew faculty from several of Harvard's schools and from many disciplines. The subject was addiction and addictive behavior, particularly among juveniles, and the effects that various early childhood programs might have on addictive behavior exhibited later in life.[36] For the first hour or so of the meeting, the social science researchers held sway, describing this study and that one, and what they could and couldn't tell from the collection of available studies (which were contradictory in some areas, and generally inconclusive in the aggregate). The moderator invited Jack Shonkoff (professor of child health and development, and director of the Center on the Developing Child at Harvard University), who had been quiet until that point, to comment. His first words were, "I wouldn't start with program evaluation. Nor would I start by talking about early preventive programs. I'd start with the science, and what we know about early brain development."

Professor Shonkoff and a colleague, Charles Nelson (professor of pediatrics), proceeded to explain to the group what they knew about the plasticity of the brain and the effects of toxic levels of stress during early childhood. Through intensive use of brain scans, the pediatric neuroscience community had been able to watch over time the different effects of too much stress, too little stress, and healthy levels of stress during the early years of childhood, when the patterns of synapses within the brain are still being formed. Natural scientists and medical experts know the value of program evaluation, but they draw on a much broader repertoire of inquiry techniques.

Ernest Nagel, in *The Structure of Science*, points out just how much has been learned by the human race through lay inquiry, careful observation, creativity, exploration, experimentation, trial and error, and incremental adjustment.

> Long before the beginnings of modern civilization, men acquired vast funds of information about their environment. They discovered the uses of fire and developed skills for transforming raw materials into shelters, clothing, and utensils. They invented arts of tilling the soil, communicating, and governing themselves. Some of them discovered that objects are moved more easily when placed on carts with wheels, that the sizes of fields are more reliably compared when standard schemes of measurement are employed, and that the seasons of the year as well as many phenomena of the heavens succeed each other with a certain regularity.[37]

Charles Lindblom pushes a little harder and questions whether we actually need social science at all. The accomplishments of the *natural* sciences and engineering, he proposes as a stark contrast, are many and obvious:

> Yet the troubling possibility persists that with no or only a few exceptions, societies could perhaps continue to go about these and other activities if social scientists vanished, along with their historical documents, findings, hypotheses, and all human memory of them. . . . The disappearance would presumably in some ways render social tasks more difficult, but perhaps in no case render any existing social task impossible, as would the disappearance of any one of many contributions from natural science and engineering. The value of social science to social problem-solving remains clouded to a degree that would shake any social scientist's complacency.[38]

My purpose in quoting these rather pointed arguments is not to dismiss the relevance of social science research methods to policing but, rather, to press the point that social-scientific experiments and evaluation constitute a relatively small and very particular subset of the relevant inquiry tool kit.

We should at least consider which natural science inquiry methods might turn out to be relevant or important for policing. A great many of them, I would suggest. Most of what we know about social problems and most of the knowledge already accumulated by police stems from the mind-set and methods of natural science inquiry: observation, inspection, investigation, and diagnosis, leading to the development of ideas about the scope, nature, and dynamics of various dysfunctions and breakdowns in the social order. Even in policing, natural science inquiry methods have a better-established and more robust record of accomplishment than social science's experimental methods.

Some sociologists and criminologists might complain that this is unfair and might protest that they themselves use many of the methods of natural science inquiry, even when examining social issues. Indeed, some of them do. Many social scientists engage in field research, case studies, observation and reporting, synthesis, evaluation, hypothesis development and testing. Many of them have an attitude of professional curiosity, conduct careful observations, compile descriptions, construct stories and derive meaning, offering insights that others may then accept or reject.

However, an elite group emerges within the discipline: the *randomistas,* as they are known in the field of development economics.[39] They argue that one cannot possibly know anything for sure without a randomized, controlled experiment. They set the standards for professional inquiry so high, and focus on such particular methods, that they then become the ones uniquely qualified to make determinations. They explain carefully to their peers, and to the rest of the world, why more casual or unstructured methods provide no substitute, and how most people, therefore, really don't know anything for sure.

In this sense, regrettably, EBP is in danger of developing as an elite science. Many of its proponents are thinly disguised randomistas, and some have no disguise at all. They focus on the most demanding levels of proof, view lay inquiry as poorly structured and, therefore, invalid, and claim the monopoly right to govern operational decisions in policing. Whatever progress had been made when social scientists learned to embrace a broader range of natural science methods is swiftly undone when the randomistas produce their hierarchy of evidence and draw threshold lines across it. They leave virtually all of the natural science inquiry methods below the line, effectively demoting them to the unacceptable category, for which there is no place within their "elite (social) science."

EBP's Scientific Methods Scale

The EBP movement has developed a five-level hierarchy, which they call a *scientific methods scale*.[40] Randomized controlled experiments belong at the highest level (tier 5), whereas mere correlations belong at the lowest level (tier 1). The threshold for acceptability is drawn at tier 3, where experimental designs include "moderate statistical controls" such as comparisons between control and treatment groups and between pre- and posttreatment: "Programs coded as working must have at least two 'level-3' to 'level-5' evaluations showing statistically significant and desirable results and the preponderance of all available evidence showing effectiveness."[41]

Hence, police programs will only be deemed proven if multiple independent studies have confirmed their effects. To be valid, the contributing "experiments and quasi-experiments should include large samples, long follow-up periods, follow-up interviews, and provision for an economic analysis."[42] EBP has also declared some willingness to consider findings from meta-studies, which compile volumes of data from multiple sources as an alternative to designing new experiments from scratch. To be acceptable, such studies must be extensive and suitably sophisticated. Such stringent specifications will surely have the effect of keeping "acceptable methods" beyond the capabilities of ordinary mortals, thereby guaranteeing a stream of social science research funding for decades to come. EBP has set its thresholds, and the vast majority of ordinary "lay inquiry" and natural science methods fall short of it.

Above EBP's threshold line (in terms of acceptable methods for establishing program effectiveness) lie controlled experiments (preferably randomized), meta-studies, and a miscellaneous collection of other sophisticated program evaluation techniques. Social scientists have one other favorite tool—regression analysis—used not so much to determine causality (as it mostly establishes correlations rather than causal linkages) but used at an earlier stage of inquiry to identify factors that might exert significant influence on specific outcomes. Identifying such factors, of course, could lead, eventually, to clues about potential interventions and policy effects. However, there would normally be a lot of ad hoc probing, prodding, and messy experimentation before a regression finding (establishing the significance of one factor or set of factors) could be translated into an intervention design. Nevertheless—and perhaps because of the sophistication and apparent ubiquitous applicability of the tool—regression analysis also seems to have earned a place in the social science elite's preferred tool kit.

Other Ways of Knowing

Perhaps it is worth bearing in mind that Sir Isaac Newton established the laws of motion and elasticity without using any of these preferred methods. Using his trademark combination of scientific curiosity and creativity, he first estimated the speed of sound in air by clapping his hands at one end of a walkway in Neville's Court (Trinity College, Cambridge) and measuring the interval between the clap and the echo returning from a wall at the far end of the courtyard. Having no stopwatch, he synchronized the swing of an adjustable-length pendulum to match the delay and later computed the period of the pendulum. He surely conducted experiments. He did so to test the theories he developed to explain the observations he so carefully made. Observation begat theories, and theories begat further observation. His experiments were neither randomized nor controlled, and involved no meta-analyses or regressions.

Perhaps it is worth bearing in mind that the vast majority of modern medical knowledge has accumulated without the use of this elite tool kit. Yes, specific remedies are now tested through randomized clinical trials, but medical students first learn anatomy and are required to dissect a cadaver as part of their training so they can see how the human body is put together. They learn how the musculoskeletal system works, then the cardiopulmonary system, the endocrine system, the nervous system, and so on. They learn about the myriad ways in which physiological failures can occur. During their training, they talk to hundreds or thousands of patients with various symptoms and conditions. They do most of this learning by using their own eyes and ears, aided by microscopes, stethoscopes, scanners of one kind or another, patient interviews and examinations, and lab tests galore.

Only at a very late stage, when the medical community

wants to check the efficacy of one treatment protocol compared with another, in relation to a specific condition or diagnosis, does it turn to controlled experiments. When it does, medicine has many advantages over policing. Throughout the world, the human body works basically the same way and is subject to common modes of failure or dysfunction. (The same is not true for societies, communities, neighborhoods, or crime problems).[43] These medical failure modes are finite in number and have already been codified as a list of diagnoses (not true for policing problems). For almost any diagnosis, there are at least thousands of cases, if not millions (not true for policing problems). For clinical trials in medicine, hundreds or thousands of patients can generally be identified who not only share the same underlying diagnosis but also satisfy any additional demographic filters experimenters may choose to apply.

Modern medicine generates numerous clinical trials, in part because of the interests of corporations. Manufacturers of drugs and medical devices have powerful incentives to overstate the effectiveness of their products and to press those claims on doctors and patients alike. Regulators (such as the U.S. Food and Drug Administration) require manufacturers to supply evidence from clinical trials before granting approval for new products or certifying new uses for them. Stringency in testing seems natural and appropriate in such circumstances, given the commercial incentives in play.[44]

Randomized studies turn out to be easier to run, as a practical matter, for drugs than for other types of medical intervention. The administration of drugs is relatively easy to standardize. As medical researchers have pointed out: "There is a lack of generalizability once we move away from drugs to manual interventions. For example, difficulty in devising practice policies in surgery arises because decisions depend on the features of a particular patient (obesity, anatomy, quality of tissue), the particular surgeon, and various external factors (equipment available, competence of assistants).[45]

What is true for surgery is most certainly true for policing, with little prospect of precisely replicating interventions across jurisdictions. The good news, in medicine, is that, for pharmaceuticals—an area where commercial propositions deserve the most careful scrutiny—the treatments happen to be relatively generalizable, which makes clinical trials feasible.

It may be good news for policing that there are relatively few commercial interests at stake in advancing one crime prevention strategy over another. We should certainly beware those cases where specific commercial products are closely associated with specific policing strategies or tactics (as may be the case with the recent emergence of predictive analytics and the adoption of technical products such as Tasers and particular types of firearms, body armor, or vehicles). Such circumstances demand heightened skepticism, closer scrutiny, and stricter evaluative standards. There do not appear to be any particular commercial interests behind problem- or community-oriented policing, so expensive research to safeguard against commercially motivated and overblown claims of effectiveness probably are not needed in these areas. Lower levels of evidentiary support for these strategies might serve the profession perfectly well.

Natural Science Inquiry Methods in Policing

Does the police profession use the equivalent of natural science inquiry methods? Absolutely. I would suggest that crime analysis, intelligence analysis, intelligence gathering, investigations, investigative field-craft, and general surveillance techniques all fall squarely into this category. These are the ordinary processes of discovery, structured and unstructured, through which police find out what is happening and why, and begin to explore how best to intervene. Such methods can be more or less sophisticated, of course, and they can be very sophisticated indeed without involving any of the tools from EBP's elite tool kit. Moreover, police and scholars can collaborate closely and productively around such methods.

The Boston Gun Project provides an obvious example of such a collaboration. Three Harvard scholars worked closely with Boston police and other agencies to find the causes of escalating juvenile homicide rates in Boston and figure out what might be done. They were given some hypotheses, developed more of their own, and tested these hypotheses by talking to street workers, gang members, and anyone else who could provide useful insights. They inherited one particular theory—that the violence was fueled by an uncontrolled supply of guns from southern states. They checked out that theory by tracing guns used in past homicides back to their point of first sale. What they found out (most of the guns used in homicides were sold first in Massachusetts and were relatively new when used) demolished that theory, and the team quickly abandoned it. Next, they searched for new ideas, listening carefully to a broad range of players. Like natural scientists running back and forth between the lab and the field, these researchers moved back and forth constantly between data analysis and street-level inquiry, each form of investigation informing, enriching, and redirecting the other. Eventually, "the structure of the knot" came into focus, and its internal dynamics became clear. The researchers and their police partners saw clearly the structure of the sixty-one gangs, the patterns of established gang "beefs," and the role played by peer pressure within the gangs when it came to violence. Finally, once they understood the structure of the problem, the project team devised a tailor-made strategy to reverse the effects of peer pressure within the gangs.

What did these researchers not do? For this project, they did not conduct any randomized experiments or perform any meta-analyses. Neither did they use regression analysis. The entire project was set up and funded (by NIJ) as a problem-solving demonstration project, not as a program evaluation or criminological research project. In fact, there was no formal experimental structure for the project, which may leave the EBP community wondering whether or not Operation Ceasefire really worked or whether the 63 percent reduction in the youth homicide rate,[46] which quickly followed implementation of the Ceasefire strategy, was merely some kind of fluke.[47] Maybe, several years later, EBP scientists will come up with some method to confirm (subject to their own standards of evidence) that Operation Ceasefire actually saved lives. Even if they do, we should be grateful for all the lives that will have been saved in the meantime.

What a shame it would be if this type of cooperation between police and scholars were not valued just because this partnership used nothing from the tool box of elite science. What a shame it would be if the many forms of analysis this team (and others like them) employed along the way while unraveling a serious crime problem were deemed unsatisfactory. What a tragedy if operational policing ever had to wait for social science to catch up.

Because some social scientists use natural science methods, and natural scientists occasionally run controlled experiments, drawing a sharp line separating the two sets of research methods is somewhat problematic. However, distinguishing the much smaller set of social science methods approved by the EBP elite from all other scientific methods is actually much easier, simply because the preferred tool box is so small and its contents quite easily enumerated.

Data Analysis and Pattern Recognition in the Natural Sciences

Some may make the mistake of assuming that natural science methods look only locally, through the microscope or by way of lab tests, at one object at a time, and that any methods involving analysis of large data sets (such as crime analysis) must obviously belong to the social sciences. This is plainly wrong. The entire field of pattern recognition techniques, for example, aligns better with the instincts of natural scientists than with those of social scientists. Fraud detection algorithms (which operate across massive databases of financial and transactional data) have nothing to do with program evaluation or controlled experimentation, and everything to do with searching for anything strange that might be there and exploring the nature of anything that appears.

Nicholas Christakis (professor of medicine and medical sociology at Harvard Medical School) explores the mechanisms through which disease or health effects are transmitted through social networks. Through the application of network analysis and other analytic methods, he has shown, for example, how obesity can be transmitted through social ties as individuals influence the attitudes and behaviors of family and friends around them. Christakis reports that the advent of social networking sites such as Facebook have presented researchers in this area with enormous repositories of data, electronically available and ripe for analysis. His use of these data sets is highly sophisticated, deeply scientific and analytical in nature. Nevertheless, his instincts align more with the mind-set and methods of investigation and exploration rather than program evaluation; hence, more with the habits of natural scientists than those of social scientists.[48]

In a recent interview with *Harvard Magazine*, Christakis explained the significance of natural curiosity and open-mindedness, coupled with a broad range of analytic instruments, in finding out how things work. He applies the same mind-set, he implied, when exploring terabytes of social network data as Galileo employed when he peered through his telescope to fathom the structure of the heavens:

> In some ways the availability of these new kinds of data is like what the microscope was to Van Leeuwenhoek or the telescope to Galileo. When the telescope was invented, Galileo just started looking at stuff. He looked at the moon and he saw mountains. He looked at Jupiter and found moons encircling it. He looked at the sun and found sun spots. There's this huge part of science which is just about careful observation and curiosity about the world.[49]

This "huge part of science" routinely dwarfs social science in making contributions to knowledge. It would be strange, indeed, if Galileo and Newton, who have taught us so much about the way the universe works, were deemed not to have engaged in "high science" simply because their methods did not rely on randomized experiments or program evaluation techniques.

There is no prima facie reason why the ratio of natural science methods to social science methods applicable to policing should differ markedly from this ratio in other areas. One can obtain a rough sense of where that ratio lies, in general, by comparing the rate at which new articles are abstracted into various academic citation indices. For the United States, the rate at which articles are being added to the general science citation indices runs at roughly five times the rate at which articles are being added to equivalent social science citation indexes.[50] Across a range of industrialized nations, this ratio varies between 5:1 and 10:1. In other words, social science may account for no more than 10 to 20 percent of new science.[51] Given that the elite tool box and preferred methods of EBP represent a relatively small subset of the overall social science tool kit—certainly less than half—then it might be reasonable to guess that EBP should represent no more than 5 to 10 percent of the investments the police profession could usefully make in scientific inquiry. From this perspective, the notion of EBP playing a central or dominant role in the relationship between police and scholars begins to look woefully unbalanced.

In discussions about police science, some commentators mention the natural sciences and engineering but they lump these together under the general rubric of devices or technologies, which they say the police are much too eager to adopt. They virtually ignore natural science inquiry mechanisms, normally the larger piece of the scientific pie, and, thus, downplay the significance of crime analysis as an example of a different type of science that is more directly relevant to operations.

Some commentators confuse crime analysis with social science. David Weisburd and Peter Neyroud observe little "involvement between scientific work in the universities and the work of crime analysis in policing."[52] Specifically, they complain: "Police departments do not encourage their scientific staff to publish in scientific journals in criminology; indeed, they generally discourage them. Science in this sense is not a part of large policing centers. The implications of this are that the scientific quality of crime analysis units is often relatively low."[53]

In other words, these authors suggest that crime analysis should involve the same type of analytic sophistication as criminological research, and any crime analyst worth his or her salt should be publishing studies in scientific journals. On this point, as on so many others, proponents of EBP seem to equate science with criminological research and ignore the significance of inquiry and analytic methods that are perfectly valuable for diagnosing crime problems and guiding operations but lie well outside the realm of criminological research.

It is quite a different thing to make the police profession "an arena of evidence-based policies"[54] rather than a sophisticated user of scientific methods. Conflating these purposes may well serve to elevate the status and interests of social scientists but would be disastrous for police. To set things more properly in balance, one might surmise that evidence-based policing, because it is unlikely to meet more than 5 percent of the police profession's overall scientific needs, should probably receive no more than 5 percent of the funding for police science and a commensurate level of attention.

If such a rule seems remotely reasonable, then the police, along with their scholarly supporters, will need to make a serious commitment to figuring out what mix of investments should constitute the remaining 95 percent of the science agenda because, so far, we have heard less about this part. It is not too hard to identify some of the priorities in this space. The police profession, aided by the scholarly community, should:

- Aim to broaden the range of crime analysis techniques available beyond the narrow traditions of spatial analysis and CompStat. We should help police understand that problems come in a daunting array of shapes and sizes, and help them to develop the broader analytic versatility required to reveal a broader range of problems and bring them into clearer focus.
- Learn more about the interplay between data mining and investigative field-craft, so that macro-level analysis and micro-level examination can each inform, refocus, and complement the other in a continuous cycle, as police seek to identify and comprehend the complex phenomena they confront.
- Continue to develop intelligence analysis techniques versatile enough to assess local, regional, national, and international crime problems (because the security threats that confront police continue to diversify and vary considerably in scale).
- Develop a clearer vision of what might constitute analytic vigilance for the profession, learning to avoid "failures of

imagination," knowing how much time and resources to spend on looking, and knowing how to look, even when there might be nothing to find.

■ Explore and import a much broader array of pattern recognition techniques to help police spot emerging, invisible, and unfamiliar problems earlier and more reliably.

■ Define and refine the (several) supporting roles for data analysis, measurement, and monitoring during the different phases of the problem-solving process.

■ Invest in the quality of analytic support available to operational policing and dramatically increase the availability of analytic services throughout departments.

■ Continue the drive to elevate crime analysis and intelligence analysis to the status of a profession,[55] taking care to prevent this emerging discipline from being confused with (or captured by) criminology or the social sciences.

All of these investments would be deeply analytical and could draw on diverse streams of scientific knowledge and scholarship.

Toward a More Stable and Sustainable Relationship

The relationship between academia and the police profession remains tenuous and vulnerable, but significant progress has been made in developing fruitful collaborations of many types. Scholars have worked with police on political management, organizational design, organizational change, police culture, training, enhancing educational standards within the ranks, and developing analytic methods as well as helping to develop operational strategies and tactics. Scholars have participated in problem-solving projects, chaired inquiries and commissions, and have served extensively as consultants to police executives.

All of this is too valuable to jeopardize. Giving evidence-based policing a central position or allowing it to dominate interactions between police and academia may stifle the relationship.

The form of the relationship proposed by proponents of evidence-based policing offers virtually no benefits for police. The best they can hope for is that the scientists they have invited in, after months or years of research work, will finally confirm what police thought they knew already: that an intervention or program the department had previously deployed did actually work. The downside risk for police is much greater. Maybe the research findings will prove to the world that police actions are irrelevant or ineffective and that apparent successes turn out to be bogus or mere luck. For police managers, what joy! No wonder many executives scratch their heads and wonder why they would want to enter into such a partnership. Meanwhile, the scholars offer police no real help with pressing operational needs because they have such a short list of approved methods. The scholars bear no responsibility for the consequences of action or inaction and feel no obligation to invent anything useful. They mostly want to evaluate.

While the benefits for police seem minimal, the costs loom large. Police must proceed more slowly, even in the presence of urgency, to satisfy the demands of experimental design. Police agencies must accommodate scholars, providing them access to staff and data and confronting the legal issues that arise when outsiders are allowed in. Police end up driving the scholars around, keeping them safe, and generally looking after them. Police executives voluntarily subject their own actions and their officers' actions to scrutiny, dealing with the associated press inquiries and reputational risks. Managers have to persuade their own officers to cooperate with researchers despite their workloads, beliefs, and worries about outside scrutiny—a task made no easier if the scholars use condescending phrases such as *high science* and *elite scientists*.

Evidence-based policing does have a place in policing, but it needs to be kept in its rightful place. EBP employs expensive and complex methodologies that need to be strategically deployed. There are many areas of policing where these methods are not, and will never be, relevant or useful. Problem-oriented policing may well be one such area. EBP should recognize that and simply leave it alone.

There are other areas where EBP's rigorous evaluative techniques seem more appropriate. Where police adopt programs or methods that are expensive, long term, potentially permanent, and that are deployed in a sufficiently standardized way across many departments, evaluating these programs with a reasonable degree of rigor may well be important.[56] With respect to a small number of major programs, EBP may deliver some value. Then again, given the substantial difficulties involved in conducting controlled experiments within a policing context, EBP might extend its disappointing track record, offering few valuable insights.

The profession should not overlook the many other useful contributions that scholars can make and that science can offer. There are many other forms of scientific inquiry, more akin to natural science methods, that need more urgent development within policing. These are more relevant to the bulk of operational policing challenges and should take priority among science investments at this time.

What is the right way to make the interaction between scholarship and practice richer and more productive? Preferably by understanding the particular and limited contributions that social science research methods can make to operational policing, and by embracing a substantially broader range of investigative, analytic, inquiry, and intelligence techniques more generally suited to the operational demands of the profession.

FIVE

Partners in the Production
of Public Safety and Security

Co-production of public safety lies at the heart of a community policing philosophy. Progressing from a professional era model (where police regarded themselves as *the* professional crime fighters) to a community policing model requires public police to appreciate and accommodate the broad range of contributions to public safety that can be made by other parties.

In the community policing model, public police become less the deliverers of security and more the orchestrators of security provision. However, we would not want public police to be naive about the motivations and professionalism of other contributing parties, even as they enter into partnerships with them. The July 2015 shooting of black motorist Samuel Dubose by a University of Cincinnati police officer (discussed in chapter 1) raised many of these concerns, especially as Dubose had no connection with the university and the traffic stop took place in a public street more than a mile from the campus.

Co-production can be especially tricky when it seeks to integrate contributions from public, not-for-profit, and for-profit organizations, all of which have differing motivations, different values, and different systems for governance and accountability. Much of the security apparatus now operating within the United States is owned and controlled by corporations, and corporate interests frequently diverge from the public interest. Even local community efforts such as neighborhood watch, if not properly governed, can end up serving the parochial interests of one group while trampling the rights of others.

The boundary between public and private policing is messy and complex. Police executives deal with some aspect of it almost every day. Private investments in security continue to expand and public–private partnerships of myriad types proliferate, even as budgets for public policing stall or decline.

This chapter provides police executives and other policymakers with an opportunity to explore the critical issues that arise at this boundary. The analysis here starts with a number of assumptions. First, that it is no longer possible for public police to ignore the extent and pervasiveness of private policing arrangements. Second, that being in some general sense "for" or "against" private security is not helpful, as such views are inadequately nuanced or sophisticated given the variety of issues at stake. Third, that the interests of private parties will rarely, if ever, be fully aligned with public interests. Fourth, that it is not sufficient for public police agencies simply to deal with the private security arrangements that exist today; rather, public police have a role to play in influencing future arrangements and in making sure those arrangements serve the public interest.

For the purposes of this discussion, private policing is broadly construed, and means the provision of security or policing services other than by public servants in the normal course of their public duties. The clients for private policing may, therefore, be public (as with neighborhood patrols) or private (as when corporations contract with private security firms or employ their own security guards).

The providers of private policing may include:

- Volunteers: Private individuals acting as unpaid volunteers (for example, neighborhood watch).
- Commercial security-related enterprises: For-profit commercial enterprises that provide some aspect of security/policing services (for example, security companies, hired guards, hired neighborhood patrols, private investigators, alarm companies).
- Specialist employees in private or not-for-profit organizations: Employees who have specialist policing, security, or risk management roles within organizations whose core mission is something other than security. These personnel may be employed by corporations as security officers, by a retail establishment as store detectives, by a private university as members of the university's own police department, or by the owners of other commercial premises (for example, shopping malls) as guards or patrols.[1]
- Nonspecialist employees in private or not-for-profit organizations: Employees with more general duties who are, nevertheless, asked to pay attention to security issues (for example, store clerks watching out for shoplifters; airline flight crews observing passengers for suspicious behaviors).
- Public police: Circumstances in which public police are paid by private clients for specific services. In some situations the officers are off duty or working overtime for a private purchaser (as with paid police details). In other cases police officers are on duty but committed to a specific policing operation paid for at the agency level by a private client (for example, policing a major sporting event).

David Bayley and Clifford Shearing's NIJ-commissioned study described the plethora of structural permutations emerging around the world at the boundary between public and private policing. They reported that the distinguishing features of the reconstruction of policing were "a) the separation of those who authorize policing from those who do it, and b) the transference of both functions away from government."[2]

Many types of structure are now familiar. We see information-sharing networks straddling the public and private sectors. We see subsets of public policing functions being contracted out to private industry. We see public police officers working for private clients under a variety of different arrangements. We see not-for-profit associations forming, with membership from public and private organizations, allied around some common security-related purpose. Public police also cooperate on a daily basis with security guards and patrols operating in privately owned or quasi-public spaces, such as shopping malls, industrial complexes, private universities, or gated residential areas. Also—this is not so new, but is, nevertheless, at the boundary of public–private policing—police routinely rely on private individuals, co-opted as confidential informants, to assist in their investigations.

Given the range of different structures, putting together reliable statistics on the overall "size" of private policing seems an almost impossible task, as any estimate will depend heavily on the definition of what is covered. One European study from 2013 estimates an overall European ratio of 31.11 private security personnel per 10,000 inhabitants—only slightly lower than the public police ratio, at 36.28 per 10,000 inhabitants.[3] In the United States, the number of private security guards overtook the number of uniformed public law enforcement officers in the early 1980s, exceeded it by 50 percent by the late 1990s,[4] and that number now is projected to grow from roughly 1 million in 2010 to 1.2 million by 2020.[5] In Australia the number of private security personnel outnumbered public police by 2006, and now the ratio could be as high as 2:1.[6] In Israel, the ratio was between 2:1 and 3:1 twenty years ago. Sklansky and others remark how difficult it is to generate valid estimates for the scale of private policing, and for a variety of reasons: private police are hard to count, their organizations have a tendency toward secrecy, statistics tend to undercount employees who have some security functions, and calculations omit altogether the increasingly ubiquitous practice of public police engaging in private duty.[7]

Background

Skillful management of the relationships between public and private policing constitutes a core competency for police executives. Realizing this and accepting it, however, has taken the policing profession a good long while, and the route followed to arrive at this point varies by country.

In the United Kingdom, public police, for decades, steadfastly resisted any association with private security. Adam White provides a detailed history of private security in Britain from 1945 onward, and reveals the decades-long obdurate refusal by the Home Office to recognize the industry.[8] The emerging industry itself—comprising mostly large firms that provided guards and security patrols for commercial premises—wanted desperately to be regulated. Regulation would signal recognition and approval, and might even provide governmental quality assurance for established firms, which they could use as a marketable stamp of approval. Establishing standards for qualification and conduct would help keep irresponsible or incompetent players out of the market, thereby enhancing the credibility and reputation of the established firms.

But the British government perceived commercial interests

and private involvement as a threat to the essential "stateness" of security provision—a belief deeply embedded in British culture, as in the cultures of Canada and Australia.[9] The concept of "stateness" reflects the view that only state (civic) institutions can be trusted to provide security while judiciously balancing the multiple and often conflicting rights of different groups or individuals. Any form of government recognition for the private industry could compromise or distort the public policing mission, and the government, even by playing the role of regulator, would be seen as taking responsibility for the conduct of an industry whose motivations and competence it regarded as inherently untrustworthy.

Things changed significantly during the Thatcher era (1979–90).[10] Thatcherism emphasized the role of free markets and advocated privatization of state functions. A belief in the merits of privatization required a higher level of appreciation for the capabilities of the commercial sector and a greater degree of trust in the ability of competitive markets to sort out the good from the bad.

The New Labour philosophy (1994–2010), espoused by prime ministers Tony Blair and Gordon Brown, carried forward many of the themes of Thatcherism, which endorsed market economics, deregulation, and privatization.[11] Public–private partnerships became all the rage as mechanisms for efficient and effective delivery of public services, and so it became natural for government to embrace private security as partners in the fight against crime.

Thus ended the British government's reluctance to engage constructively with the private security industry. For the London Olympics in 2012, the contract with G4S, which was at that time the world's largest international security corporation, was so extensive that the "bungling" of the contract—when it became clear that G4S could not provide enough guards—

became an international spectacle and led to the resignation of G4S chief executive Nick Buckles.[12]

According to White, the United States was never so concerned with "stateness" and always displayed a greater appreciation for the role of commercial enterprise.

> In the USA private security companies are able to act as ordinary commercial organizations selling ordinary commodities—their activities do not seem to be structured by state-centric expectations about how security ought to be delivered. . . . deeply embedded capitalist free-market ideology . . . seems to permeate most aspects of American life, including the domestic security sector. This ideological persuasion means that market signals in the American domestic security sector are not bound up with moral and normative considerations as they are in many other countries.[13]

Greater cultural acceptance of private policing does not mean, of course, that concerns do not arise. Concerns arise in the writings of legal, constitutional, and democratic theorists seeking to clarify what societal aspirations the United States should hold, even if its history is different. Concerns arise as a result of failures, scandals, and abuses in the industry, each instance of which provides another opportunity to appreciate the risks associated with private policing. Concerns arise when new technologies in the hands of private actors affect civil liberties or privacy in ways that ordinary citizens had not anticipated or imagined. Concerns arise as private policing continues to grow apace, becoming ubiquitous and touching the lives of ordinary citizens on a daily basis.[14]

Concerns that have arisen, and which have been discussed in the literature, include the unnecessary use of force, abuses of power, denial of access to public spaces, dishonest business practices, unequal access to security provision, and weak accountability mechanisms for private agents. Nevertheless, as Elizabeth Joh explains, prevailing official attitudes in the United States have portrayed such problems not as "fundamental faults inherent to private policing, but technical issues amenable to improved regulation."[15] Many of these criticisms, after all, are often directed at public police agencies also. But Joh, in her examination of private policing, expresses surprise at the superficial nature of the attention that concerns about private policing have received: "What is striking, however, is that even in embryonic form, these concerns hardly register in discussions about partnerships, which . . . are typically presented with unalloyed enthusiasm."[16]

Other commentators point to subtle problems that relate very specifically to the character of private policing. Gary Marx, as long ago as 1987, pointed out the importance of *revolving door* effects:

> The [private security] industry, particularly at the more professional and leadership levels, is composed of thousands of former military, national security, and domestic police agents for whom public service was a revolving door. Some federal agents leave when they face mandatory retirement at age fifty-five. Many local police retire at a relatively early age after twenty years of service. However, limited mobility opportunities and more lucrative private-sector offers attract many others long before retirement.

These agents were schooled and experienced in the latest control techniques while working for government, but are now much less subject to its control. They may also maintain their informal ties to those still in public policing. An insurance company executive, in explaining the rationale behind hiring former police officers for investigative work, notes that if the latter cannot gain direct access to the needed information, "there are their friends." This "opens up the doors for us so we can work both sides of the street."[17]

Marx referenced organizations such as the Association of Federal Investigators, the Society of Former Special Agents of the FBI, the Association of Retired Intelligence Officers, and the International Association of Chiefs of Police. He stated that such organizations may create "formal and informal networks that serve to integrate those in public and private enforcement,"[18] and questions whether former government agents (whom one might normally expect to be better skilled and more publicly oriented than those with no public sector experience) employed in an investigative capacity by private firms should, in fact, face greater restrictions and registration requirements as a result of the specialist knowledge and access they acquired through public service. They might know how to hide improper investigative techniques from discovery by public authorities. They might retain high levels of expertise in surveillance. Their "old boy networks" might provide improper access to information and intelligence.

At the leadership levels, private security firms may hire senior ex-FBI or Secret Service agents or former police chiefs as directors or as other senior executives. In part, no doubt, it is their skills and experience that these private firms value. But such appointments also serve to cloak the for-profit enterprise with a veneer of public spiritedness, as well as provide strong personal links into the law enforcement establishment.

Marx and, more recently, David Sklansky have examined another set of concerns related to the fact that private police agents, being constitutionally classed as citizens (unless officially deputized), can legally do things that public police cannot.[19] For example, there is no constitutional protection against unreasonable search and seizure by private citizens. There is no requirement for private security agents to issue Miranda warnings. There are no exclusionary rules for evidence obtained through unauthorized searches or questioning conducted by private agents. These factors might heighten anxiety about private agents who could be highly skilled (such as ex-government agents) but subject to less stringent legal constraints and less effective oversight than their public service counterparts.

We might also worry, but in a rather different way, about private security agents who are untrained, unqualified, or unprofessional, or those who use unethical practices or excessive force. The affront to civilized society that the behavior of such agents provides may be less subtle and more visible to ordinary citizens. Law enforcement officials often complain about private police as "untrained, unprofessional, unregulated and unaccountable police wannabes that simply get in the way of 'real police work.'"[20]

Marx also raised concerns about the extensive deployment of police details for private clients: "During off-duty hours public police may serve as private police. . . . In many big city departments such employment is a jealously protected perquisite. Some departments in effect run private businesses out of headquarters. While operating on behalf of private interests they have all the powers of sworn agents and may even drive official patrol cars."[21]

Within the United States at least, such concerns—subtle or otherwise—have never been sufficient to make any serious dent in the general enthusiasm for commercial private security. The industry grew rapidly, beginning in the late 1960s. "Partnership" was established as the basis for interactions between public and private policing beginning in the 1970s.

Ethical issues raised are treated as peripheral concerns in the

United States. The primary motivation is to control crime, now generally recognized as too extensive and complex to be dealt with by public police alone. Governments have moved "beyond passive acceptance to active encouragement," trusting that, for the sake of getting more help, they can overcome the problems associated with the profit motive in commercial security.[22]

Recent terrorist incidents illustrate and emphasize the importance of security collaboration across the public–private sector divide. Joh notes increased emphasis on public-private partnerships in the post-9/11 world, with contributions of private security guards regarded as essential components of critical national infrastructure protection.[23] In the wake of the Boston Marathon bombings in 2013, investigators made extensive and very public use of video surveillance tapes provided by commercial entities (as well as photographs and video provided by members of the public) to identify and track suspects.[24]

In 1976 a report on private policing commissioned by the Law Enforcement Assistance Administration declared "the sheer magnitude of crime in our society prevents the criminal justice system by itself from adequately controlling and preventing crime."[25] Since then, Joh observes that the notion that private security could serve as *"equal partners* with the public police in the co-production of security, rather than simply as subordinates providing a complementary service" has gained prominence.[26] One could interpret this shift as reflecting a maturing of the ideals of community policing, wherein the police and the public (including private firms) work collaboratively to set the security and crime-control agenda and then to carry it out.

Bayley and Shearing also point to a more complex range of partnership arrangements that go beyond the outsourcing of specific police functions: "The change in policing cannot be understood in customary terms. It is often mischaracterized, for example, as 'privatization.' Because the distinction between public and private domains becomes problematic in the new policing, the more appropriate description for what is occurring is 'multilateralization.'"[27]

The Law Commission of Canada, in a 2013 report, likewise signals a deeper kind of symbiotic and networked set of relationships:

> In the last several decades, we have seen the extraordinary growth of the private security sector, offering a wide range of services. However, it is not simply the case that private security is filling a void left by the public police. Today, it is more accurate to suggest that policing is carried out by a network of public police and private security that is often overlapping, complementary, and mutually supportive. Within this context, it is increasingly difficult to distinguish between public and private responsibilities.[28]

So private policing is here to stay, "warts and all." It just needs to be managed. As Bayley and Shearing conclude: "It is important for governments to continue to safeguard justice, equity, and quality of service in the current restructuring of policing. To safeguard the public interest in policing, governments must develop the capacity to regulate, audit, and facilitate the restructuring of policing."[29]

Values at Stake

A substantial body of literature discusses the pros and cons of a variety of private policing arrangements and recounts the shifting attitudes of public police toward private security over time. Academic literature has focused slightly more on the cons, with particular emphasis on threats to democratic governance, procedural protections, civil liberties, and human rights.[30] By contrast, government inquiries and reports seem to accept the rise of private policing as inevitable and focus more on how public police should best exploit and manage the partnership opportunities presented.

Much of the debate as to whether, why, and how much society should worry about any specific private policing arrangement has focused on a finite number of core issues. It would take too long to trace these issues through all the relevant literature, so this chapter does not take on that task. I simply assert the claim (which others may dispute) that the major issues summarized in box 5-1 (presented as five categories of benefits to be derived from engagement with private policing and seven categories of risks) cover the vast majority of such debate. Of the seven types of risk, the first five represent threats to society at large and the last two represent risks that more specifically affect public police and police agencies.

Notice that number 3 on the benefits side (Greater Equality in Protection) and number 5 on the risks side (Greater Inequality in Protection) both refer to the issue of equity in access to security, and the resulting effects on the level of protection for the poor and vulnerable. That argument can be made either way. Most often in the literature, however, growth in private policing is perceived as increasing inequity and, thereby, harming the poor. For example, a 2009 report commissioned by the International Peace Research Institute in Norway observes:

> One of the ironies of private security is that it is least affordable by the very neighbourhoods that tend to need it the most. . . . [Private security thus] serves the interests of wealthy and ruling elites. . . . Privatized enclaves are in a sense an

Box 5-1. Potential Benefits and Risks of Public–Private Police Partnerships

Grounds for Support and Engagement (Benefits)

1. **Increased Effectiveness through Public-Private Partnerships.** Collaboration between public and private sectors enhances performance by sharing complementary skills, knowledge, and resources. Partnerships facilitate information exchange and provide access to broader networks. All parties can benefit from properly functioning partnership arrangements.

2. **Alignment with the Ideals of Community Policing.** Community policing is essentially collaborative and involves sacrificing a purely "professional" agenda in favor of one negotiated with the community. The community, which includes businesses, should be able to participate in setting the crime-control agenda and should be encouraged to participate in carrying it out.

3. **Greater Equality in Protection.** The ability of the better-off to protect themselves by purchasing private protection at their own expense allows the public police to concentrate their efforts on poorer and more vulnerable segments of the community. The overall effect, therefore, is to raise the floor in terms of levels of protection for the most vulnerable.

4. **Access to Specialized Skills and Technical Resources.** The private sector can provide the public police with highly skilled and technical specialists that the public sector could not routinely employ. Collaboration with the private sector thus makes highly skilled and specialist resources available for public purposes.

5. **Efficiencies through Contracting Out.** Government operations should seek to exploit the efficiencies of

private-sector competitive markets by contracting out any components of their operations that can be clearly specified and carved out, and for which competitive markets exist.

Grounds for Skepticism and Concern (Risks)

1. **Lack of Accountability.** Private police are not subject to the same formal and legal systems of accountability that govern public police agencies. Nevertheless, they may carry weapons, use force, detain suspects, and intrude on the privacy and rights of individuals. They may discover crimes and choose not to inform public authorities. The exercise of policing powers without commensurate accountability is inherently dangerous to society.

2. **Threats to Civil Liberties.** Many restrictions on the conduct of public police do not apply to private police (unless formally deputized by public agencies). For example, confessions extracted by private police without Miranda warnings and evidence obtained through unlawful searches conducted by private agents are not subject to exclusionary rules.

3. **Loss of "Stateness."** Policing services and security operations require judicious balancing of the multiple and often conflicting rights of different groups or individuals. Therefore, only state ("civic") institutions can be trusted to reflect the broad societal values required to carry out such functions. The particular interests of private clients and the for-profit motivations of commercial providers will inevitably distort the public agenda to some extent.*

4. **Threats to Public Safety.** Private police, who are not as well-trained as public police, may display poor judgment or overreact to situations, thus endangering public safety. Citizens may be confused about the status or rights of

*Several of these concerns, including loss of equity in public security and loss of public accountability, appear as separate items on this list.

Box 5-1. Potential Benefits and Risks of Public–Private Police Partnerships (Cont.)

uniformed security personnel, and may, therefore, act in ways that create danger for themselves or others.

5. **Greater Inequality in Protection.** The growth of private security exacerbates inequality regarding citizens' access to protection. Citizens will get the level of protection they can pay for. Those who are better off and able to purchase or enhance their own security will reduce their commitment to public policing. Funding and support for public policing will suffer, which will ultimately result in lower levels of protection for the poorer and more vulnerable segments of society.

6. **Reputational Concerns.** Inadequate performance or improper conduct by private security personnel may produce reputational or litigation risk for public police if the public police have formally recognized, qualified, trained, contracted, or in some other way recognized or validated the operations of private operators. Such operators should, therefore, be kept at arm's length.

7. **Threats to Police Jobs.** Increased availability of lower-skilled and lower-paid security jobs, coupled with the contracting out of some police tasks to the private sector, may undermine job security and limit career prospects for public police. Competition from the private sector is inherently unfair because of its tolerance for lower training standards and access to cheaper labor.

abandonment of the public realm in security. They represent a "secession of the successful" from the rest of society.[31]

Four Scenarios

The Executive Session group discussed the subject of private security at the June 2013 meeting at Harvard, using hypothetical scenarios specially prepared to serve as the basis for discussion. These four hypotheticals illustrate common dilemmas and challenges that confront police executives while avoiding the potential embarrassment that could arise from naming any particular police department or private organization. The chiefs of police present said that these hypotheticals were each perfectly plausible. In fact, several were eager to recount (under the Session group's conditions of confidentiality) equivalent or similar situations from their own experience. It also became clear, as the discussion proceeded, that each scenario raised a different combination of benefits and risks to be recognized and managed.

These four scenarios are presented here. The set of four is also available as a stand-alone document from the National Institute of Justice (without commentary) for use in a training environment.[32] Using these hypotheticals as a basis for classroom discussion would provide police executives with an opportunity to think through the benefits and risks that accompany various types of public–private engagement, and to practice using the specific decision sequence they would need to use in a real-life operational setting when similar situations arise. Such exercises might enhance or speed up issue recognition and diagnostic skills.

To speed up the analysis, an instructor may choose to provide students with a copy of the summary listing of issues culled from the literature in box 5-1 to prime them regarding the various benefits and risks to look for. Alternatively, participants could be left to work out for themselves, from scratch, what the relevant concerns might be.

Decision Sequence

Public police examining any private policing arrangement, existing or proposed (and no matter how complex), might follow these basic steps:

Step 1: First, work out the potential benefits for the public. In particular, be clear where the interests of the private parties involved actually align with, and therefore could be expected to advance, the public interest. Look for the benefits listed in box 5-1. Does the scheme bring more players, more technical expertise, or increased resources to existing public purposes?

Step 2: Work out what the accompanying risks or threats are for the public. Look for the types of risk listed in the table. Be specific about the ways in which public interests and private interests diverge. Expect to discover that public–private alignment of interests can vary considerably on different matters, even in the context of one specific partnership. Alignment can be good on some issues and bad on others at the same time, even between the same organizations.

Step 3: Work out what could be done through the actions or influence of public police (as well as through possible enhancements to regulation, oversight, or accountability) to mitigate the specific risks identified in step 2.

Step 4: Weigh the benefits and risks, forming an opinion on whether the scheme, on balance, can be defended and promoted as being in the public interest.

Step 5: If it can be defended and promoted, clarify the lines of argument that should be used to support the overall scheme, as well as the actions required by public police to mitigate the accompanying risks. If it cannot, clarify the lines of argument that public police should use to oppose or resist it.

There is nothing particularly novel in this decision sequence, but it might help provide some structure for police executives when they are thinking through complex situations of this type. (This five-step template could readily be used as "study questions" for group discussion of the hypothetical scenarios in a training environment.)

Note that this analytic sequence does not provide the kind of *bright line* that some officials wish to draw—a line that would neatly separate those functions that must always be public from those that can be private. The idea that public and private security provisions are already deeply intertwined and interdependent makes discovery or specification of such a line seem implausible.

Rather, this analytic route uses a different bright line— identifying, for any proposed interaction, the issues on which public and private interests will be well aligned while, at the same time, carefully identifying the other issues where public and private interests will naturally be at odds. Deriving the benefits of alignment while dealing with areas of potential conflict goes right to the heart of the challenge of managing partnerships effectively.

Scenario 1: Elite Hostage Rescue Unit

You are chief of police in a major U.S. city. The country's military budgets are shrinking, and many military units withdrawn from Afghanistan face demobilization. Members of an elite special-forces unit, formerly based in your jurisdiction, have set up a new commercial venture offering a range of security services. The company, SafeConduct, has established its headquarters adjacent to a local airstrip and operates two executive jets and two helicopters. It offers executive hostage rescue services through major international security companies, working mostly abroad.

However, the company always has at least one "team" at home (that is, not deployed abroad). The CEO of SafeConduct offers to provide armed containment and hostage rescue services for your department on a "time and materials" basis. Fees would be charged only upon deployment, and there would be no costs to the city for training or for maintaining readiness.

Readiness, the CEO promises, is not an issue. SafeConduct could guarantee a team on site anywhere within your jurisdiction within three hours of notification. The company would provide its own communications system and would, for every deployment, provide a unit commander to act as liaison with police Incident Command. All its unit members have extensive operational experience in Afghanistan and elsewhere and are proud that they have not "lost a hostage" in their past ten deployments.

Your own hostage rescue unit (a subunit within your SWAT team) spends two days per month training for this role, but has been deployed for hostage situations only four times in the past three years. (SWAT is deployed more often, of course, to deal with a broader range of incidents involving armed, or potentially armed, offenders.) None of the officers currently assigned to the hostage rescue unit has been involved in more than two actual hostage rescue operations.

A deal with SafeConduct would save the city substantial costs involved in training and maintaining your own hostage rescue capability. SafeConduct teams would participate in training exercises as required (on a time and materials basis). SafeConduct's CEO is prepared to offer these very favorable terms because, given the nature of the work the company does, he views good working relationships with law enforcement and security agencies as a critical strategic asset.

The CEO hands you a recent press clipping from England, which describes the four "tough tests" that the British Labour Party recently proposed for deciding which aspects of police work should be contracted out.[33] Any deal with private contractors should: represent value for money; ensure security; be transparent and accountable; and foster public trust in the police service. He says he is confident that this proposal easily passes all four tests, especially considering the experience and skills of SafeConduct's personnel and the favorable financial terms he is offering.

Discussion of Scenario 1: Elite Hostage Rescue Unit

In the Executive Session discussion of scenario 1, the police chief officers present were troubled mostly by the issue of accountability, especially in relation to the use of potentially deadly force. If a public police agency deployed a private firm, the public agency would remain accountable for the operations of that firm. In complex and dangerous situations, it seems unlikely that the public agency could exercise effective command over the military unit. The need to exercise effective control would be particularly acute in this case because use-of-force doctrines differ markedly between military operations and civilian law enforcement. Military units are more oriented toward the use of decisive force against enemies and less toward apprehending violators and achieving peaceful resolution. The police chiefs at the Executive Session were quite uncomfortable with the prospect of being accountable for something they felt they could not adequately control.

This scenario also raises questions regarding which parts of the policing function can reasonably be contracted out. The four criteria proposed by the British Labour Party are certainly relevant, but not sufficiently demanding. In contracting out policing functions we also have to worry about "stateness." Contracting out clearly definable tasks (such as servicing vehicles, monitoring alarm systems, or staffing turnstiles at a sporting event) seems quite different from contracting out tasks that require careful balancing of competing interests, the exercise of judgment in determining the public interest, or the use of force against citizens. Having private contractors perform carefully circumscribed guard duties seems more obviously acceptable than having them deal with domestic violence calls or attend to neighborhood disputes.

Public agencies should contract out only those functions that pass all of the following tests:[34]

1. The services to be purchased are clearly definable and separable from other duties of the public agency.
2. Unambiguous performance standards can be set, and the public agency has contract oversight staff qualified to and capable of monitoring and enforcing those standards.
3. A series of graduated sanctions can be applied to the contractor, through contract provisions, to correct any instances of poor performance. (This avoids the "all or nothing" trap when the agency's only recourse is to take the difficult step of canceling a contract.)
4. An efficient and competitive market exists for the services being purchased (this guarantees value for money and prevents the agency from being stuck with an underperforming provider due to a lack of viable alternatives).
5. The market price for the services is lower than the cost to the agency of providing the services itself.
6. "Stateness" is not an issue, as the service does not require the use of complex judgments about competing interests or the use of force against citizens.
7. Profit motives, coupled with the contract pricing struc-

ture, will not produce perverse incentives. (If such distortions seem likely, then item 2 becomes of paramount importance in counteracting biased incentives.)

SafeConduct's proposal fails to satisfy conditions 2, 4, and 6. If SafeConduct's elite unit is better trained and more experienced than agency personnel, it seems unlikely that clear performance standards could be established and maintained, especially during a high-intensity operation. In the absence of a competitive market, once the agency has disbanded its own hostage rescue unit, it may become too dependent on the one available supplier. Also, for the reasons already discussed, public police executives will not be comfortable being held accountable for something they cannot sufficiently control.

From box 5-1, the most relevant risks for this scenario are 1: Lack of Accountability, and 3: Loss of "Stateness." The proposal could also pose risk 4: Threats to Public Safety, given the differences between military and civilian use-of-force doctrines.

The proposal brings benefits, too, as it might produce 1: Increased Effectiveness through Public–Private Partnerships, 4: Access to Specialized Skills and Technical Resources, and 5: Efficiencies through Contracting Out.

Participants in the Executive Session discussion, even while they were unwilling to accept the proposal as offered, were eager to find a way to realize these benefits. (As one police chief commented, "I wouldn't kick this one to the curb.") They discussed possible variations of the proposal, such as buying training from SafeConduct and renting technical equipment, while ensuring that the use of force in operational settings remained the preserve of public police officers.

Given the infrequent nature of hostage situations and the highly specialized nature of the related training, participants were also keen to realize efficiencies of scale. To do that, they wanted to explore other mechanisms, such as the creation of regional consortia, shared services models spanning multiple jurisdictions, or even buying specialist services from a bigger police department close by—all mechanisms that would preserve the essential "stateness" when it came to the use of deadly force.

Scenario 2: Neighborhood Watch

You are chief of police in a major U.S. city. The population of the city is racially diverse, but largely segregated at the neighborhood level. Your community outreach program collaborates on a formal and frequent basis with twenty-seven Neighborhood Watch Associations (NHWAs), which your program officers helped establish.

Your deputy chief, who is African American, has an eleven-year-old son, Jason. Jason has told his dad that he and all the other black kids in the Montvale neighborhood no longer dare walk through Compton—a predominantly white neighborhood—on their way to and from school. The quickest route from Montvale to the (newly integrated) school lies through three pedestrian walkways that pass under the highway separating the two neighborhoods. The Compton NHWA patrols have apparently set up checkpoints close to these walkways and question any kids who pass by, sometimes asking them to open up their backpacks.

The Compton NHWA patrols openly carry weapons. The state has a "stand your ground" law. There have been no reports of violence or of the Compton patrols actually using physical force. But, clearly, the Montvale schoolchildren are intimidated and many have chosen to use longer routes to school, adding at least fifteen minutes to their journey each way.

Your senior management team has discussed the situation.

Your general counsel advises that the neighborhood patrols, provided they do not use physical force, are merely acting as private citizens and have not committed any offense. Also, they cannot be held accountable should their patrol patterns suggest racial bias, because they are not public police and have not been formally deputized. Counsel advises the only legal remedy lies in civil lawsuits.

The captain in charge of the community outreach program has discussed the situation with the Compton NHWA coordinator, who denies any racial bias and reports that focusing on schoolchildren passing through has eliminated a significant rash of late-afternoon domestic burglaries in the Compton neighborhood. Your CompStat director confirms this was a growing problem and that it evaporated over recent weeks.

In the wake of the Trayvon Martin tragedy, twenty of your twenty-seven NHWAs have voluntarily agreed to stop carrying weapons and to strictly limit their activities to an "observe and report" role. Your deputy has suggested an urgent policy change, whereby the department would officially and publicly dissociate itself from any NHWAs that choose not to adopt this restriction.

While you are considering your options, you also learn from your public relations officer that the Montvale NHWA, who also openly carry weapons, are incensed by the intimidation and humiliation their children have suffered and are considering escorting their children through Compton in the mornings and afternoons. The city's major newspapers want to know how your department plans to deal with the deteriorating situation.

Discussion of Scenario 2: Neighborhood Watch

The second scenario illustrates many of the dangers associated with vigilantism and aggressive neighborhood watch patrols.

The literature on private policing and security clearly alerts us to these dangers.

Sharon Finegan warns, in a 2013 article, that "neighborhood watch members wield significant authority, but they lack the training and limitations to which police are subject."[35] Finegan proposes statutory controls that would limit the ability of neighborhood watch members to confront suspects and would mandate training and expand exclusionary rules to bar the admission of evidence seized illegally by private citizens engaged in law enforcement activities.

But using regulation as the mechanism for protecting civil liberties might be fraught with difficulties, even if such legislation could ever pass. Neighborhood watch is often conducted by volunteers, many self-appointed or belonging to loosely formed informal networks. An "association" might not actually exist in any formal sense, and would, therefore, be hard to control through regulatory oversight. Moreover, the introduction of stringent requirements might deter many volunteers. Hence, the only controls generally available might, indeed, be those pertaining to the conduct of ordinary citizens.

Finegan also points out that the procedural rules and law used to limit racial profiling by police do not extend to private security companies nor to ordinary citizens. Companies may train their staff to be unbiased, but such training is unlikely to reach neighborhood watch groups:

> Burdened by (and perhaps unaware of) their own individual biases, coupled with the lack of procedural safeguards or training, neighborhood watch members may act on their biases and target individual suspects on the basis of race or ethnicity. . . . While more and more private actors are performing the tasks previously associated with police officers,

constitutional safeguards have not been extended to the conduct of private actors.[36]

In the scenario, several risks are clearly apparent. The relevant ones from box 5-1 are:

- Lack of Accountability: As the police department's general
  counsel observes, the only forms of legal accountability—
  those pertaining to private citizens—are not adequate for
  governing the behavior of the neighborhood patrols.
- Threats to Civil Liberties: Armed patrols searching backpacks and intimidating schoolchildren to the point where
  they will choose circuitous detours rather than risk an encounter are clearly not acceptable.
- Loss of "Stateness": We clearly cannot trust the neighborhood watch volunteers in Compton to balance the multiple
  and conflicting rights of different groups or individuals.
  They are totally focused on the security concerns of their
  own community and pay little heed to others' rights and or
  the importance of any broader public tranquility.
- Threats to Public Safety: The situation is deteriorating,
  and the treatment of the Montvale children by Compton
  patrols is producing genuine hostility between communities and could even lead to conflict between armed groups.
- Reputational Concerns: The police department, by virtue
  of its working collaboration with the neighborhood watch
  groups, becomes at least in part responsible for their conduct.

It is evident that this situation scores very heavily on the risk
side, triggering five of the seven major categories of concern.
But it also shows some potential benefits, which may include
increased effectiveness in crime control:

- Benefit 1: Increased Effectiveness through Public-Private Partnerships, and engagement of the community in setting the agenda and achieving results, and
- Benefit 2: Alignment with the Ideals of Community Policing

Clearly in this scenario the risks outweigh the benefits. But that does not necessarily mean that the police should automatically dissociate themselves from any patrol groups whose tactics seem unacceptable. They should not (like the general counsel) throw up their hands and say, "We have no legal way to control them." The police, by virtue of their relationship with these groups, can exert influence over them and use that influence to reestablish public priorities.

Police might emphasize with these groups, and with the broader public, that protecting life and liberty takes precedence over protecting property, and that to get any support from the police department a group formed to protect a neighborhood should also take responsibility for preserving safety and protecting civil liberties within their neighborhood and for anyone passing through it. Otherwise, that group's mission is inherently unbalanced and not sufficiently public. The police might even make it clear that they will intervene whenever the actions of a neighborhood watch group elevate one neighborhood's concerns at the expense of a broader and more balanced public agenda, or endanger public safety through the exercise of poor judgment.

Scenario 3: State Safety Association

You are chief of a U.S. state police department. The governor's chief of staff calls to ask your opinion of a proposal that has been presented to the governor by a consortium comprising three large security companies that, between them, share 80 percent of the private security industry revenues for the whole state. They propose to establish a state safety association as a vehicle for enhanced collaboration between the private security industry and public police. The governor believes in the value and effectiveness of public-private partnerships and has championed their use in many areas of public policy.

Under the plan, members of the proposed state safety association would be able to:

- Send selected employees to various courses offered by the State Police Academy and have them certified by the academy as proficient in the relevant subjects.
- Publicly display the phrase "Member of the State Safety Association" on their insignia, documents, and websites.
- Develop a deeper collaboration with the state police and other local police agencies in the form of threat-based intelligence-sharing networks.

Each company would pay a substantial annual fixed-fee subscription in the form of unrestricted revenue for your academy. Each would also pay variable fees per student for each course attended by its staff, with fees set high enough to be an attractive financial proposition for the state. All the details, of course, remain open to negotiation.

All three members of the consortium have recruited retired senior police officers to sit on their governing boards or hold executive-level positions. The largest company hired your predecessor (the former chief of state police), whom you know well, as its CEO. All three companies profess their commitment to public safety and their desire to make major and high-quality contributions to public security.

When the idea first surfaced, police unions were vehemently opposed. In a public statement, the Patrolman's Association president declared, "Corruption is defined as the abuse of public resources for private gain. Using the resources and staff of the State Police Academy to advantage private for-profit commercial companies fits the bill exactly. Such a deal would be blatantly corrupt."

Noting union opposition, the consortium members then offered to include the provision that each member company within the association would be obliged to offer paid details for off-duty state police officers at an aggregate level not to fall below 5,000 hours per year per company. "This would be valuable," a consortium spokesman said, "to guarantee the quality and depth of the relationship. The presence of public police officers on company projects will enhance the professionalism of our own staff and keep us focused on critical public purposes."

The governor is eager to understand your views. Several other security companies have complained to the state's Commerce Department that this scheme would disadvantage smaller and newer players within the security industry and constitutes anti-competitive trade practice by the "big three."

Discussion of Scenario 3: State Safety Association

On its face, the proposal to create a State Safety Association may score some points in the benefits column—1: Increased Effectiveness through Public-Private Partnerships, 2: Alignment with the Ideals of Community Policing, and possibly 4: Access to Specialized Skills and Technical Resources.

The specific benefits of the proposal are all rather obvious: better training for private security personnel, substantial financial support for a public training facility, enhanced information and intelligence sharing across the public-private divide, and the prospect of enhanced effectiveness through operational collaboration between public police and members of the association.

However, the proposition described threatens to seriously

muddy the waters between public and private interests and, thereby, presents some significant and rather subtle threats to the "stateness" of security provision—risk 3: Loss of Stateness.

All the risks associated with revolving door situations are evident. Public police executives might find their loyalties to old colleagues (now in corporate roles) in conflict with their public responsibilities. They may have trouble saying no when they should. Some police officials, contemplating their future prospects and potentially lucrative career options, might be tempted to grant favors or simply get too close to the commercial companies' for-profit agendas.

This scenario also serves to remind police executives that large corporations are sophisticated when it comes to strategy. One of the participants in the Executive Session commented, "You can deal with the neighborhood watches . . . you may be even able to deal with the business improvement districts and the universities you've got, but can you deal with these multi-billion-dollar companies that are going to come in and offer you deals, and all the rest of it, and you really think you're still in control?"

Forming an association of the "big three" established firms and creating a substantial financial hurdle for entry (the requirement to provide an unrestricted subsidy to the police college) could well be designed as an anti-competitive strategy, a way of marginalizing or creating a disadvantage for newer and smaller companies. The use of insignia that signal the government's blessing creates significant reputational risk for those public agencies and public officials involved (risk 6: Reputational Concerns).

The union first cries foul, worried that private agents given the same training as public police could no longer be denigrated as poorly trained substitutes for real police (risk 7: Threats to Police Jobs). The union at first seizes the moral high ground ("this is corruption") but is then placated when the corporations offer a bribe in the form of a lucrative package of paid details for public police officers.

Perhaps the most worrying aspect of this proposal is that there seems to be no way out of the arrangement, no available *exit*. The corporations would have it so. The police college will become dependent on the corporate funding stream. The revolving door will keep turning. The lines between public and private purposes will become increasingly blurred. Also, when an important decision looms that finally reveals the misalignment between public and private interests, the public decisionmakers may find themselves compromised, too deep in the muddied waters to extract themselves and pursue a clear public agenda. This is how corruption in the public sector often begins.

Clarity regarding public policing purposes demands some reasonable distance between public and commercial agendas. It seems just fine, highly desirable, in fact, for public agencies to engage with private organizations through partnerships governed by suitably crafted frameworks and protocols. But public police who become inextricably intertwined with commerce, as with this proposal, would seem to be asking for trouble in the long term.

Scenario 4: Private University Police Department

You are chief of police in a major city on the west coast of the United States. The campus of a private university lies entirely within your city limits. The chief of the university police department (UPD) answers directly to the university's general counsel, who answers directly to the university president. The relationship between your department and the UPD has always been excellent.

Street robberies in the vicinity of the campus have increased significantly over the past three years. Many victims are university students. Attacks, many of them involving a weapon, have occurred both on and off campus. Students are routinely advised not to resist and to give up their possessions if confronted. Most of them do so, and robberies have involved few injuries and no fatalities. However, in one assault that occurred off campus, two female Chinese students were badly beaten with tire irons and are now hospitalized with serious injuries. Detectives have suggested that these particular students might not have understood what their attackers were asking for.

Your public relations officer has been fielding media inquiries about this particular attack. She asks for your advice because she has been asked by her counterpart at the UPD to play down—or, preferably, not mention at all—that the victims were students at the university. The UPD press officer has stressed that there was really no link between the crime and the fact that these were university students, given the off-campus location where the attack occurred.

Your public relations officer shows you the latest annual Clery Act report from the university.[37] An appendix shows figures that clearly reveal an escalating trend in robberies and reported rapes over the past three years. But the text of the report fails to mention those phenomena and presents a reassuring picture of a safe environment with declining overall crime rates. Your public relations officer also shows you a recent article from a student-run newspaper, prompted by the trend in the rape figures. Student reporters had interviewed the university's general counsel, who said rates remained very low compared with national averages and that he believed the rise in the complaint rate was a direct result of a campaign run last year by Student Welfare and Advisory Services, which encouraged sexual assault victims to come forward to university authorities.

Apparently the university's admissions office has been getting more and more inquiries about campus safety from college advisors at feeder schools. Also, with the local economy in the doldrums, the university has been aggressively pursuing foreign enrollments, particularly from Asia, and would not want any publicity that directly linked the university with this recent and particularly vicious attack, or with the escalating pattern of assaults and robberies in the vicinity. The college has just mailed its annual batch of admission offers and wants to avoid any adverse publicity, especially publicity that might reach China. Such adverse publicity could lower the yield on their offers.[38]

Discussion of Scenario 4: Private University Police Department

This scenario provides a clear reminder that public and private interests can be well aligned with respect to some issues and very poorly aligned (even diametrically opposed) with respect to others. What that means, in practice, is that a specific public–private relationship (in this case, the relationship between the public police agency and the private university police department) might provide opportunities for fruitful collaboration—benefits 1: Increased Effectiveness through Public-Private Partnerships, and 2: Alignment with the Ideals of Community Policing—at the same time as it may endanger the public interest when non-aligned public and private agendas become entangled—risk 3: Loss of "Stateness."

This occurs often in other regulatory domains, where a regulated industry's incentives align with public purposes in some areas but not in others. In civil aviation, for example, business interests and public interests align extremely closely on flight safety issues. A major plane crash is not only a human tragedy; it is also a business catastrophe. Airlines, if held culpable for a crash, often go out of business, are taken over, or at least have to change their name. The business costs of a safety failure are enormous. Hence we see, quite naturally, on safety issues, a rather close and collaborative working partnership between regulators and the regulated.

But what about consumer protection issues for airline passengers? Should we trust the airlines' private incentives with respect to practices such as aggressive ticket pricing, gouging consumers with excessive or unexpected baggage fees, imprisoning them too long in planes on the tarmac, endangering their long-term health by providing inadequate leg room,[39] or making it impossible or inconvenient for them to use their frequent flyer miles? On these and other consumer protection issues, the more the airlines can get away with, the more profitable they become.[40]

Similarly, in banking regulation, the nature of the relationship between regulators and the regulated varies by the type of risk. Prudential regulation (ensuring the solvency of financial institutions) serves the long-term interests of the banks as well as the stability of the overall financial system. By contrast, on consumer protection issues (for example, cheating customers, deceptive marketing, imposing excessive fees) the relationship is more naturally adversarial, as public and commercial interests diverge.

Considering the nature of the relationship between public and private police, Joh puts this beautifully:

> Private police neither work under the direction of the public police, nor cooperate fully even when the public police would wish them to. Instead, private police managers cooperate with the public police when doing so serves their interests or, more specifically, their clients' interests. Thus, passive non-cooperation is also an important aspect of the relationship between the two groups.[41]

When scenario 4 was discussed at the Executive Session, several of the police chiefs present guessed that this scenario had been fashioned based on the conduct of specific universities within their jurisdictions. In other words, the general features of this story (putting aside the precise details) seemed commonplace. I would argue that the tensions described in this scenario will always be commonplace, simply because they are perfectly natural and, therefore, predictable. They still have to be managed, of course.

On issues of safety, both on and off campus, the interests of public police and the private interests of the university are almost perfectly aligned. Less crime is good for everybody and public police and university police will, therefore, work quite well together toward that end. If they do disagree on crime control, the disagreements will more likely be about the suitability of means than about the desirability of ends.[42]

But what about transparency regarding levels of crime? Here the interests diverge markedly. The public interest demands full and free disclosure, without any bias or editorial framing, so that members of the public—including students and prospective students—can know the risks, adjust their actions accordingly, and properly assess the performance of relevant policing agencies (both public and private).

But the university, particularly when trying to attract students, has a natural and strong interest in painting a rosy picture. University police may, therefore, be tempted to downplay, de-emphasize, or even mask reality. That explains the need for federal legislation (Clery Act, 1990) that governs the frequency and nature of disclosures regarding crimes on or near university campuses and involving university students. Regulation was *not* necessary to make the university care about safety, but regulation *was* required to make them care about transparency.

The lesson for public police is clear. You don't have one relationship with any private policing organization; you have different relationships with them on different issues. On some matters they are your natural allies, and interactions will be cordial and cooperative. On other issues, you must treat their motivations with suspicion, expect to see something less than full disclosure, and be prepared to intervene when they adopt tactics that endanger public safety, threaten civil liberties, or pursue private interests at the expense of the broader public good. There will always be some issues where their interests are diametrically opposed to the public interest. Public police need to be adept at recognizing those areas, be prepared to enforce compliance with regulatory requirements, and take it upon themselves to act in a way that will rebalance the public agenda.

Conclusion

Private security and private policing have become inescapable. It is no longer useful for public police to hang on to their own regrets about these trends, bemoan their loss of market share, or pretend that public-private partnerships cannot be useful. There are too many reasons to embrace the idea that private contributions can and should contribute to public purposes.

But that does not mean that the risks associated with private policing can be ignored. Grounds for concern remain. Our conclusion must surely be that each one of these grounds for concern, and each situation in which they arise, represents work to be done by public police. The police profession should treat these concerns as policy and operational challenges to be managed, rather than as grounds for disengagement.

As public police engage in partnerships and networked relationships involving private and not-for-profit organizations, they become less the deliverers of security and more the orchestrators of security provision. Public police need to understand clearly the motivations and capabilities of each contributor, develop an understanding of the whole system and what it provides, and do their utmost to make sure that overall provision of security squares with their public purpose.

As one Executive Session participant put it:

> Public leadership requires you to be able to lead and manage public functions, both with the operational capacity you've got and with the wider operational capacity you need. That's the test of public leadership . . . if you keep wanting to only do policing through people who report to you, who you can discipline, and you can hire and fire, we're dead, we're never going to get the job done.

Taking responsibility for the overall provision includes taking responsibility for the distribution of protection across society. It is the responsibility of public police to monitor the quality of security in different neighborhoods, to find out who is well protected and who is not, and to find a way to address the deficits.

It is also the responsibility of public police to look ahead—to pay attention not just to the parts of traditional police functions that they might lose, but also to be prepared to explore new areas that public police have mostly left to the private sector. Law enforcement has engaged relatively little with identity fraud, financial fraud, health care fraud, other white-collar crime, and Internet-based crimes. Security threats, familiar and unfamiliar, will surely demand an expanded repertoire of collaborative arrangements.

It is my hope that this chapter provides a clear framework that police executives can use to examine their interactions with private policing and to determine more readily how to maximize the benefits to society while minimizing the associated risks.

SIX

Partners in the Art of Risk Control and Harm Reduction

This chapter is an invitation. The police profession has much to gain by recognizing its kinship with a broad range of regulatory professions. Developments in policing theory and strategy would move much faster if the police profession recognized the kinship and joined the regulatory fold.

Social regulators of virtually all types wrestle with analogues of community and problem-oriented policing. These other professions may use different vocabulary, but they all debate regularly what kind of relationship they should foster with the industries they regulate: how much they should trust; how much of the work can be shared or delegated; and how to balance the use of enforcement methods with a broader range of less coercive compliance and behavior modification tools. They are also keenly interested in the value of organizing around specific problems, trends, issues, risk-concentrations, harms, and patterns of noncompliance. Several of them use or have used the term *problem solving*, while others use alternate phrases such as *operational risk management, harm reduction approaches,* and (more recently) *risk-based regulatory practice.*

Law enforcement agencies, security and intelligence organizations, and social regulatory agencies all exist primarily to protect society from a variety of harms. Such harms include crime, pollution, occupational hazards, transportation hazards, corruption, discrimination, various forms of exploitation, food contamination, terrorism, and risks from unsafe commercial products. The core task for such organizations is to identify harms, risks, dangers, or threats of one kind or another, and then either eliminate them, reduce their frequency, mitigate their effects, prevent them, or suppress them; and, by so doing, provide citizens with higher levels of safety and security.

Agencies with risk-control tasks at the core of their mission are a special breed and can learn much from each other. They are fundamentally different from the other half of government, which provides citizens with *services*, such as education, health care, welfare, or public transportation systems.

Enforcement and regulatory agencies accomplish their task principally by constraining the behavior of citizens or industry. They deliver protection from harm primarily through the delivery of obligations, and they use the coercive power of the state to back up that delivery. They may, on occasion, restrict business practices, seize property, suspend licenses, and even deprive individuals of their liberty or life. Not surprisingly, given their use of such powers, these agencies are scrutinized and criticized more for their uses and abuses of power than for their uses and abuses of public funds. The price paid by society in terms of governmental intrusion, loss of liberty, and imposed restrictions has to be worth it in terms of risks reduced, harms prevented, or dangers mitigated.

The vogue prescriptions used to improve governments' performance over the last thirty years, largely imported from the private sector, have provided little instruction in relation to these distinctive risk-control tasks. The management guidance available has focused on customer service, business process improvement, and quality management,[1] and much less on the challenges of operational risk control, behavior modification, compliance management, or the structuring of enforcement discretion around specific harm-reduction objectives. Risk-control agencies have been left to fend for themselves, to invent their own more particular brand of reforms, and to seek more specialized and relevant sources of inspiration.

For more than a decade, Harvard has been convening executive programs designed for exactly this group of regulatory professionals, with the express purpose of focusing on those managerial and organizational dilemmas that they all share and that separate regulatory and enforcement agencies from the remainder of (mostly service-providing) government.[2] A few police executives have attended these courses and quickly discovered a natural kinship with their regulatory peers. But the number of police executives attending remains relatively small, as most police professionals do not view themselves as "regulators" nor do they recognize regulatory strategy discussions as relevant for the police profession. Some years ago, we even altered the name of the course, to "Strategic Management of Regulatory *and Enforcement* Agencies," in a deliberate attempt to emphasize the relevance for police and other law enforcement agencies, but to relatively little avail.

Historically, the police profession has paid little attention to literature on regulatory strategy, drawing insights instead almost exclusively from dedicated studies of policing and from the academic disciplines of criminal justice and criminology. The police profession seems to have operated on the maxim "If it is not about us, it is not for us." What this means, in effect, is that most good ideas for improving regulatory strategy have to be invented twice, once for social regulators and then again (and usually independently) for the police profession.

Occasionally criminologists make the connection, drawing parallels between different fields. When they do it is usually instructive, opening up experience gained in one field to a much larger audience. For example, in 2012, John Eck and Emily Eck illustrated the potential value for police in glancing sideways to see what their regulatory peers are up to and what tools and methods they may have developed. Their paper "Crime Place and Pollution" compared the regulatory methods environmental agencies use to control industrial pollution with the methods police might use to control crime patterns spilling outward from a bar, nightclub, casino, or other establishment.[3]

Eck and Eck explore a variety of control instruments, more normally associated with environmental protection, that might become relevant to crime control if we view crime as an externality emanating from specific places (badly managed bars, clubs, or poorly protected parking lots), and where the consequences (costs) of the resulting crime-clusters are borne by other patrons, local residents, or persons in the vicinity. The question then becomes how best to induce place managers to take more responsibility for controlling the crime problems associated with their businesses or premises. With that goal in mind, Eck and Eck consider the use of penalties (for failing to implement mandated controls), subsidies (to encourage deployment of relevant technologies), tax reductions (as rewards for contributions to control), and rating schemes (to inform consumers of the levels of risk). They also question whether issuing tradable permits to place managers, specifying amounts of crime to be expected or accepted in the vicinity, could conceivably produce the same kind of efficiency gains in crime control as in the control of industrial emissions.

The application of such ideas to crime control is certainly

interesting and worthy of deeper consideration. Many of the particular methods that Eck and Eck propose in this particular paper would probably not hold up, as the authors seem to anticipate, in the face of potential ideological objections. From the victim's perspective (imagine a vehicle owner whose car is robbed overnight in a parking garage), it would be difficult to understand what it meant that this particular crime was "within the permitted amount of crime" or what the policy justification was for permitting any crime at all. With pollution, at least there is some countervailing benefit, as industrial pollution results from the socially useful processes of energy production and industrial manufacturing. Hence, society accepts the fact that pollution, although it still needs to be controlled properly, is neither inherently evil nor completely avoidable.

From the place managers' perspective, treating local crime problems as an externality produced by their businesses might seem objectionable and legally questionable. Eck and Eck neatly summarize their central assertion thus: "Places can emit crime just as a coal-fired power plant can emit sulfur dioxide."[4] From a legal perspective, this analogy may turn out to be awkward. Place managers would no doubt point out that sulfur dioxide has no brain, exercises no choice, and, therefore, cannot be held responsible for the damage it causes. Even with evidence of place-centered crime-clusters, obvious difficulty remains in attaching responsibility to the owner or manager of a premises for crimes committed elsewhere, and usually later, by their patrons—who, of course, exercise considerable choice in the matter and are fully responsible for their own behavior.

My point is not at all to dismiss any of these options, nor to downplay the value of making such comparisons. Quite the opposite, in fact. Such comparisons do a great deal to stimulate the tactical imagination, but picking and choosing from a range of regulatory instruments needs care and attention and a lot more discussion. Obliging businesses to pay experience-rated premiums into a crime compensation insurance scheme—in the same way that businesses are obliged to buy workers' compensation insurance from the state, with premiums based on their own recent occupational injury rates—might provide suitable financial incentives for better control. Admitting evidence of local crime patterns at license renewal hearings also seems plausible and defensible. In any case, finding ways to re-internalize the externalities associated with criminogenic places is a worthwhile pursuit and might produce some novel approaches. I will look forward, as such work matures, to someday parking my car in a hotel parking lot next to a sign that proclaims, "Hotel management takes full responsibility for any damage to, or theft from, vehicles parked in this lot."

What Explains the Divide?

Given the natural kinship that police should by virtue of their mission feel with other regulators, and the many benefits that could result from exchanging ideas and tools, it is worth wondering why police have not, to date, joined or enjoyed the broader brotherhood of harm reduction professionals.

Several factors contribute to this. First, police do not view themselves as "regulators" because they are not involved much, if at all, in the promulgation of regulations. Police rely on existing criminal statutes for their legal authority and seldom generate subsidiary ordinances or regulations in the way that most social regulators do.

Culturally, police agencies seem distinct, too. They wear uniforms, carry firearms, and traditionally exhibit many aspects of a quasi-military culture. They feel greater kinship, therefore, with other law enforcement agencies that share these same features (for example, Customs, Coast Guard, and Immigration) than they do with their unarmed, nonuniformed, unsworn civilian counterparts in regulatory agencies.

The domain for police work also is different. Police often seek *persons unknown* and *at large* for crimes committed. Their jurisdiction is everywhere, covering both public and private spaces. By contrast, much of the work for other regulators focuses on specific business premises or plants. Officials responsible for management of the plant and compliance with regulations are clearly identifiable, up front. Their behavior might be an issue, but generally their identity is not.

Also, the risks police tackle have some distinctive properties. Many involve opponents (criminals or perpetrators) who seek deliberately to evade detection and adapt their strategies to circumnavigate control initiatives.[5] Most environmental problems and workplace safety hazards do not have that property. If occupational safety regulators identify a safety hazard accurately and address it, then that hazard does not go searching for some other way to kill people! If environmental professionals solve one pollution problem, they do not generally create another. Most environmental, health, and safety hazards have no brain, and, consequently, they cannot deliberately seek to thwart official efforts to control them, nor do they try to hide their activities. Criminal enterprises clearly do both.

Curiously, during the last few years, environmental regulators have been running more often into problems that do, indeed, involve conscious opponents. Such problems include illegal logging, poaching, or smuggling of endangered or protected species; deliberate and illegal introduction of sport-fish into lake systems where they do not belong; and the increasing involvement of organized crime groups in toxic waste management (and illegal dumping). In all these areas traditional environmental regulatory approaches seem weak and not quite appropriate. The underlying scale of such problems is unknown, as most illegal activity is deliberately hidden. Displacement occurs when regulators intervene. The regulatory job becomes, suddenly, much more dangerous. And environmental regulators now have to consider the use of a broad range of tactics and methods—such as undercover operations, covert surveillance, and the use of paid informants—that they almost never used in relation to pollution problems originating from industrial plants.

Where might environmental professionals go for advice on such matters? They need to go to police and other law enforcement professionals whose risk-control responsibilities routinely involve tackling opponents (thieves, hackers, smugglers, or terrorists), and who frequently use such tools and methods. Law enforcement agents could readily help environmental professionals understand the role that intelligence and counterintelligence play in such situations, the importance of unpredictability and mystery, and the justifications for official deception in combating criminal enterprise. The potential learning, if police talked more often with their regulatory counterparts, would surely go both ways.

Common Ground

Some significant differences are, indeed, worth noting. Such differences can provide a rich source for discussion across disciplinary lines. But the commonalities are far more numerous and more important, and the strategic and organizational dilemmas these professions confront are strikingly similar.

Law enforcement agencies and agencies of social regulation exist primarily to control harms of one type or another.[6] They are expected to be effective in providing protections but also be minimally intrusive and burdensome at the same time. They all use reactive, preventive, and proactive methods and seek to integrate these into coherent control strategies.

In terms of organizational forms, they each run specialist functional units and operate core high-volume operational processes as well (responding to calls, processing tax returns, reviewing license applications and renewals, and taking complaints), but they also want to organize themselves to deal with specific risks or problems, even when these problems do not align neatly or at all with existing functions, processes, or any other piece of the established organizational structure. The police profession calls this problem-oriented policing, whereas many regulatory agencies talk of risk-based regulation or (in tax administration) compliance management.

These agencies all want to understand how to deploy analysis to help identify and disaggregate risks more accurately and how to orient their performance story around harms reduced, risks controlled, or problems solved, rather than around traditional output or activity measures. They all contend with inevitable tensions that arise between competing values, where organizational effectiveness seems to require the use of careful targeting, selection, and focus, but that seems fundamentally at odds with the traditional regulatory values of consistency, uniformity, equity, and fairness.

They are all expected to embrace the values of openness, predictability, and transparency, but they have to somehow square those values—especially when dealing with conscious opponents intent on thwarting control efforts—with their need to remain on occasion unpredictable, to use disinformation or deception (as in undercover operations), and to retain the element of surprise.

These agencies also wrestle with the foundational dilemmas of regulatory policy, such as the tension between the *legal* model of regulation (where regulators focus on procuring compliance with existing law) and the *expert* model of regulation (where regulators focus on harm reduction and invent alternative methods for influencing behaviors that may be harmful but not illegal). The regulatory world at large is currently leaning more explicitly and deliberately toward the *expert* model. Reasons for this include increased public pressure for better protection in the wake of the attacks on September 11, 2001, the global financial crisis, and other perceived "regulatory failures." The burgeoning risk literature (which naturally focuses more on risks than on noncompliance) might have helped, too, although the risk sciences literature has focused more on the psychology of risk perception (by individuals) than on risk control as a governmental or organizational challenge. For sure, the modern focus on risk and risk control has helped inspire regulators to focus more carefully on the business of identifying and suppressing specific harms, especially emerging and unfamiliar ones, rather than continuing to rely on traditional processes and programs.

Explicitly acknowledging and embracing the expert model constitutes a profound shift. It affects virtually every aspect of modern regulatory conduct. Currently, regulatory executives are grappling with the implications for organizational structure, managerial decisionmaking, the use of discretion, the structure of performance reporting, and the evolving nature of their relationships with the communities they regulate.

All these issues affect police organizations, too. Police use somewhat different vocabulary to describe them. What police call problem oriented, other regulators call risk based. What police call community policing looks remarkably similar to what regulators call coregulation—signaling closer, collaborative relationships between government and people, and shared responsibility for establishing and pursuing a risk-control agenda.[7]

Potential Benefits

The police profession could benefit in many ways from joining regulatory strategy discussions. First, they would discover a much broader range of compliance management and behavior modification techniques (regulatory instruments) than police have used traditionally, several of which might be applied usefully to crime control and other public safety issues.[8] Second, police would observe a more carefully delineated set of regulatory structures, as they figure out, with respect to any specific risk, who should be responsible for which parts of the risk-control task.

We can learn a lot about alternative regulatory structures and the ways in which they relate to the idea of risk management by crudely splitting any risk-control initiative into three parts. For a specific risk to be controlled (whether it relates to crime, pollution, disease, or safety hazards), someone has to identify the risk, someone has to analyze the risk and design a suitable intervention (analysis and design), and then someone has to act in a particular way or stop acting in particular ways to apply the intervention. Regulators and the regulated community can split these three tasks between them in various permutations and combinations, and—depending on which parts of the job government keeps and which parts government delegates to the community—thereby produce distinct models of regulatory interaction.

Under the traditional regulatory approach (model 1 in figure 6-1), government retains responsibility for spotting risks, analyzing them (maybe with some consultation along the way), and developing an intervention design. Government then issues prescriptive rules or regulations informing the community what must be done to control the risk (for example, "Balconies must be equipped with railings at least three feet high and with bars no further apart than four inches"). The regulator focuses thereafter on procuring compliance, and compliance with the rules is assumed necessary and sufficient to control the risk. Regulators call this prescriptive or rule-based regulation. Those who disapprove of this style of regulation have also attached to it a variety of derogatory labels, including command-and-control regulation and one-size-fits-all regulation.

When regulators recognize diversity in the regulated industry, they shift to model 2, delegating the analysis and design parts of the risk-control task. In other words, government still identifies the important risks but allows the community considerable flexibility in how it will control them. In the regulatory literature, this approach is usually called performance-based, outcome-based, or principle-based regulation.

Delegation does not necessarily stop there. Large companies in highly technical arenas press for more control. They argue that it is they, not government, who know their own business best and employ the best technical experts, and, therefore, they are in a better position than government to identify the relevant risks. High-tech industries thus press for control of all three parts of the risk-control process: risk identification, analysis and design, and intervention. Model 3, where the regulated industry or community takes responsibility for all three, is called self-regulation. Under this model, industry is basically relied on to run its own risk management operation, and the role of government regulators changes significantly. Now they get to approve industry's risk management plans up front, and, subsequently, they audit the operations of the risk management system on a periodic basis to make sure the company is effective in identifying and controlling risks. They also should maintain their own independent audit and discovery systems so they can verify the truthfulness of the company's account regarding problems that appear and their success (or failure) in controlling them.

FIGURE 6-1. Regulatory Structure: Four Models

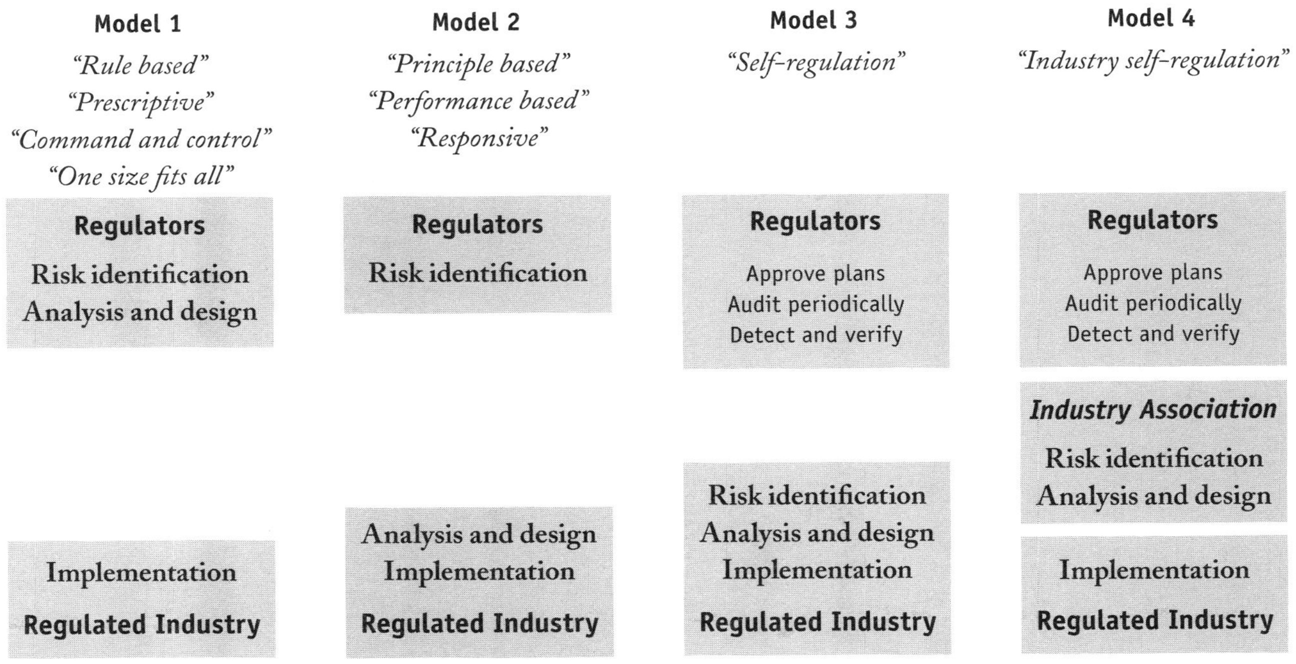

Model 1

"Rule based"
"Prescriptive"
"Command and control"
"One size fits all"

Regulators
Risk identification
Analysis and design

Implementation
Regulated Industry

Model 2

"Principle based"
"Performance based"
"Responsive"

Regulators
Risk identification

Analysis and design
Implementation
Regulated Industry

Model 3

"Self-regulation"

Regulators
Approve plans
Audit periodically
Detect and verify

Risk identification
Analysis and design
Implementation
Regulated Industry

Model 4

"Industry self-regulation"

Regulators
Approve plans
Audit periodically
Detect and verify

Industry Association
Risk identification
Analysis and design

Implementation
Regulated Industry

Model 4, industry self-regulation, is a variant on model 3. Some industries, particularly those consisting of a large number of small companies, do not want the bother of designing and running elaborate risk-control systems at the company level. But they do not want government imposing burdensome and prescriptive rules, either. So they club together and form an industry association, which they then rely on to identify risks common across the industry, analyze and design interventions palatable to the association's members, and issue requisite guidance and instruction. One could conceivably imagine an association of bar owners or parking-lot management companies playing a similar role with respect to the types of place-based risks discussed by Eck and Eck.

In the regulatory world, models 3 and 4 have lately become fashionable. The "better regulation" movement in Europe and throughout the Organization for Economic Cooperation and Development incorporates an underlying ideological (and often political) preference for "light-touch, self-regulatory approaches." The advent of safety management systems in civil aviation throughout the world also delegates much more responsibility for risk identification and control down to the level of corporations (airlines, aircraft maintenance operations, and aircraft manufacturers), with aviation safety regulators focused increasingly on auditing the safety management systems of the industry, rather than on doing much of the risk management work themselves.

To prefer one or another of these structures on ideological or political grounds turns out to be a huge mistake. Each structure works well for specific types of risk and likely will fail if applied to the wrong sets of risks. The state of the art, in terms of regulatory design, is to begin to appreciate the need to operate multiple regulatory structures simultaneously, even with respect to the same industry, but for different classes of risk.

Self-regulation (model 3) works well for risks that are observable from the level of the corporation; that the corporation would be happy to disclose if found; that are within their capacity to control; and where controlling the risk is closely aligned with their business interests. But that is a relatively small subset of risks, and arguably it is the subset likely to be best controlled already. Self-regulation is an unreliable approach for dealing with risks that would not be visible from a decentralized perspective (that is, that require higher-level analysis and monitoring), which they would not disclose or address responsibly (such as corruption on the board or at senior levels of management), or are beyond their capacity or not in their interests to control.

The array of structural options gets more complex when two other factors are introduced. The first involves recognizing that any of these three crude phases of the risk-control process (identification, analysis and design, and implementation) can be shared rather than being placed unambiguously with government or the community. The second involves recognizing the multi-tiered jurisdictions that pertain to many regulatory tasks. Designing regulatory structures in Europe has been complicated substantially by the advent of the European Union as a regulatory superstructure. In the United States, most regulatory and law enforcement tasks involve federal and state agencies, as well as city and local departments. These additional dimensions enlarge substantially the range of options as one considers who should be responsible for which parts of the risk-control task.

In fact, as the range of structural options increases, this simple diagnostic device becomes more valuable, as it provides considerable clarity. For any specific category of crime problems, it makes sense to ask, "For *this type* of problem, *who* should be responsible for *what*?" Who is best placed to identify emerging patterns and trends? Who has a vantage point at the right level—not too high and not too localized—and the relevant data or monitoring capabilities that will enable them to spot emerging trouble, of this type, in a timely fashion? Who is best placed to analyze and understand an emerging risk and to propose suitably tailored interventions? Which parties within the community can be trusted to play their part because it is in their interests to do so, and which parties must simply be told what must be done and forced to comply (model 1) because their private interests relating to this type of risk simply do not align with public purposes? Also, which parts of the community should be consulted in the analysis and design phase because of the special insights they might have into the genesis or dynamics of specific crime problems?

Note that these questions have no right answer in general, as there is no single regulatory structure that is good for all risks. These questions have to be asked for each distinct set of risks and should lead to different arrangements in respect of different problems. That is part of what it means to master risk-based regulation.

The professional era of policing, in terms of the nature of the relationship between police and the community, most closely resembles model 1, prescriptive regulation. The community policing movement shifted the profession closer to model 2 and explicitly incorporates the notion of co-production, with responsibility shared between the police and the community for risk identification, prioritization, solution design, and delivery.[9]

Empowering communities to become crime-resistant and resilient in their own right may yet move crime control closer to model 3, self-regulation. We also might imagine that models 3 and 4 could help public policing develop constructive and appropriate relationships with a proliferation of private policing and security organizations. Where competent private organizations exist—such as security operations in an industrial park or housing complex, or university campus police departments—public police might end up assuming the role of overseers or auditors of someone else's crime-management and safety plan. Police might take a similar approach to major trucking firms or coach companies in relation to traffic compliance and highway safety. As public policing seeks to make better sense of the growth of private policing, it might be useful to explore a more diverse set of structural relationships with private parties that could end up supporting and furthering the public risk-control task.

Recent experience among regulators suggests it is best not to prefer any one model. Rather, the considerable range of possibilities should be embraced and appreciated. Tailor the choices to specific classes of risk, recognizing that any one group of actors can be your natural and trustworthy allies in relation to one problem and yet can have diametrically opposed interests in relation to another.

Unfinished Business: The Maturation of Problem-Oriented Policing

A broader look across professional lines also might shed light on the nature of progress made to date in the development of problem-oriented policing. Regulatory agencies confront problems of many different shapes and sizes, and each regulatory profession tends to have its own tradition in terms of which shapes, or dimensions, it recognizes readily. Police have focused most naturally on place-based concentrations of crime—a tradition that stretches back before the advent of geographic information systems or computerized crime-mapping software.

Other regulatory professions have different traditions. Consumer product safety focuses most naturally on the risks associated with specific products (for example, baby walkers and the associated risk of toddlers in baby walkers tipping over and falling down stairways) or with specific categories of products that pose more generic dangers (for example, plastic products made in China with unacceptably high lead-content levels).

Occupational safety regulators traditionally have focused on industry groups and categories of hazard that are concentrated within each industry group, for example: "falls from heights" and "trench cave-ins" in the construction industry; "tractor rollovers" and "deaths in grain handling" (asphyxiation of farm workers in grain silos) in farming; asbestosis in the roofing industry; lacerations to hands and forearms on poultry production lines; and so on.

Tax agencies tend to organize their compliance-management efforts around categories of taxpayers, which they call "market segments" (for example, personal, small business, big business, and international business) and then around the methods of tax avoidance or evasion that exist within particular segments.

But all regulators discover, sooner or later, that risks come in many shapes and sizes, and whereas some align neatly with existing organizational structures and well-practiced operational methods, most do not. The challenge, then, is to produce the flexibility and fluidity that enables the agency to organize itself differently for different types of risk and to do so without a series of wrenching reorganizations.

Nowhere is this challenge more acute than in environmental protection, as environmental risks come in so many different forms. Some pollution problems concern specific discharges from specific industrial facilities (and these fit nicely into traditional permitting programs, which are organized by media: air, water, and hazardous waste). But other environmental risks involve endangered species, or the arrival of exotic plants or animals that distort the equilibrium of native ecosystems. Some environmental problems are industry-specific (for example, heavy metals as a by-product of the printing industry; gypsum as a by-product of phosphorus extraction; excessive use of certain pesticides in citrus farming; or the use of mercury in dentistry). Some problems relate to topographical areas (air-basins or watersheds) where pollutants accumulate. Non-point-source pollution (like agricultural runoff) has to be monitored and managed in terms of watershed areas and permissible loadings in rivers and streams. Other problems relate to the loss of or danger to natural resources (wetlands, habitat, fish stocks, or coral reefs). Other environmental risks—such as radon gas, lead paint, mold, and asbestos—appear in the home and have nothing to do with industrial facilities and not much to do with geography.

In learning about the multidimensional character of harms and exploring the organizational challenges of a problem-solving approach, the police profession enjoyed a substantial head start, thanks to Herman Goldstein. From the 1970s onward, Goldstein addressed explicitly the limitations of geographic and temporal analysis, and the profession's reliance on standardized tactics.[10] As discussed in chapter 2, Goldstein urged police to recognize the many other ways in which crime problems might be concentrated (repeat offenders, repeat victims, classes of victims, methods of attack, patterns of antisocial behavior, and so on) and encouraged the profession to move beyond its traditional "hot-spot" focus and directed patrol responses.

More than three decades since Goldstein began teaching the policing profession about the myriad varieties of crime patterns and the importance of generating creative and tailored responses, it is worth asking how much progress the profession has made in moving beyond "cops on dots" strategies. With many departments still relying on CompStat processes and with predictive policing resting rather squarely on the idea that one can extrapolate from historical patterns to determine, in advance, where and when a crime is likely to occur, the answer might well be, somewhat depressingly, "not so much."

Even the scholarly champions of evidence-based policing, in their efforts to determine whether problem-oriented policing really works, seem to have ended up focused heavily on evaluating place-based intervention strategies. That might be because that is what problem-oriented policing has become, and, therefore, these are the only types of problem-oriented strategies widespread enough to be susceptible to systematic evaluation. For all the scholars and practitioners who have taken Goldstein's message to heart and tried to make it work in practice, these conclusions would be terribly disappointing and frustrating.

With respect to the multidimensional nature of harms, I am not suggesting that other regulatory agencies have it any easier. They just have it *different*; and differences are both interesting and instructive. Regulatory agencies vary enormously in terms of the shapes and sizes of problems they naturally recognize and are accustomed to tackling.[11] They also respond organizationally in different ways when problems come to light that do not fit their analytical and operational traditions. Some of them, particularly agencies of environmental protection, have wrestled for much longer and more explicitly with the challenges posed by pollution issues defined in different dimensions—no doubt because of the extraordinary range of problems they confront. Environmental agencies have at various times reorganized around the dimensions of the most pressing problems of the day. That just makes other problems *not fit*. At other times, they have constructed dedicated units for each different type of problem and have tried to run them all simultaneously, but that becomes expensive as the types of problems proliferate over time. More recently, many regulatory agencies are producing their own version of a problem-oriented approach, relying on fluid resource allocation and temporary risk-based project-teams, which can be formed and unformed as problems appear and get resolved, and without any need for change in the underlying organizational structure.

A Multitude of Opportunities

A richer conversation between law enforcement and regulatory agencies could bring other benefits, too. Some important harms straddle jurisdictional lines and require interagency cooperation. An obvious example is the issue of violence in the workplace, a substantial proportion of which stems from domestic disputes spilling over into the workplace. This issue clearly is a policing matter, but—insofar as it affects the safety of workers within their workplaces—it is an occupational safety concern as well. Collaboration between environmental agencies and police around the problem of toxic waste dumping by organized crime would certainly run more smoothly if these agencies became more aware of their similarities and a little less focused on their differing traditions.

The police profession also might gain from an examination of the different ways in which other regulators use science. The fields of environmental protection, food and drug safety, occupational safety and health, nuclear safety, and transportation safety are all deeply embedded in the natural sciences. Agencies employ significant numbers of highly educated scientists, with backgrounds in physical, chemical, biological, and engineering sciences. Given this strength in the natural sciences, these professions instinctively perform a detailed analysis of the mechanisms through which harms occur. A precise diagnosis of the problems up front leads naturally to highly targeted and specific interventions carefully designed to alter or interrupt precursor event sequences.

These natural science–rich agencies rely much less on social-scientific methods applied after the fact. They end up, therefore, with a different balance between natural science and social science support. They invest much more heavily in the diagnosis of problems up front, using the inquiry methods of the natural sciences, and they need much less after the fact in terms of program evaluation. They derive their confidence that specific interventions worked not so much from statistical analysis and controlled experiments, but instead from being able to study closely the mechanism of the harm and observe directly when they have sabotaged it successfully.

The police profession, as it seeks to advance its problem-solving expertise, might benefit from adjusting the ways in which it uses scientific inquiry. Hopefully, police will become more careful and deliberate up front in diagnosing the precise nature of specific crime problems and fathoming the mechanisms through which they unfold, and a little less quick to assume that the answer lies in accepting or rejecting generic programs invented elsewhere.[12] Such a shift would lead the profession to ratchet up its investments in more versatile and sophisticated forms of crime analysis in support of risk-based or problem-oriented policing.

The police profession has toiled unnecessarily because of its isolation. Joining a richer cross-professional discussion would accelerate its development. The profession does not need to invent everything for itself. Many other regulatory professions face equivalent pressures, share similar aspirations, wrestle with the same tensions and conflicts, and are exploring reform ideas perfectly applicable to policing. Hopefully this chapter has touched on enough potentially fruitful areas to make the prospect of such broader discourse seem attractive and worthwhile.

Notes

Chapters 2, 4, and 5 have been adapted with permission from papers by the author published in the New Perspectives in Policing series (Washington: U.S. Department of Justice, National Institute of Justice) as follows: "Measuring Performance in a Modern Police Organization," March 2015; "Governing Science," January 2011; and "Managing the Boundary between Public and Private Policing," September 2014.

Chapter 3 incorporates extracts from a paper by the author in the New Perspectives in Policing series: "One Week in Heron City: A Case Study—Teaching Note," September 2009.

Chapter 6 has been adapted with permission from a paper, "Crime Reduction through a Regulatory Approach: Joining the Regulatory Fold," published in *Criminology and Public Policy*, May 2012.

Chapter 1

1. Matt Flegenheimer, "For de Blasio, Attack Comes amid Tension over Police," *New York Times,* December 20, 2014.

2. Richard Pérez-Peña and Mitch Smith, "Cleveland Judge Finds Probable Cause to Charge Officers in Tamir Rice Death," *New York Times*, June 11, 2015.

3. Howard Koplowitz, "Walter Scott and Child Support: Did the Threat of Jail Contribute to His Death?," *International Business Times,* June 16, 2015.

4. Shooting of Walter Scott, Wikipedia (https://en.wikipedia.org/wiki/Shooting_of_Walter_Scott).

5. Mark Berman, Wesley Lowery, and Kimberly Kindy, "South Carolina Police Officer Charged with Murder after Shooting Man during Traffic Stop," *Washington Post*, April 7, 2015.

6. A "good shooting" is one in which it is established that someone's life was at risk, thus providing justification for the shooting.

7. For an assessment of the accuracy and completeness of the various federal collation systems relevant to arrest-related and in-custody deaths, see Michael Planty and others, "Arrest-Related Deaths Program: Data Quality Profile," Technical Report (U.S. Department of Justice, Office of Justice Programs, Bureau of Justice Statistics, Washington, D.C., March 2015), NCJ 248544 (www.bjs.gov/content/pub/pdf/ardpdqp.pdf).

8. Kimberley Kindy, Marc Fisher, and Julie Tate, "A Year of Reckoning: Police Fatally Shoot Nearly 1,000," *Washington Post*, December 26, 2015.

9. Ibid.

10. Jon Swaine, Oliver Laughland, Jamiles Lartney, and Ciara McCarthy, "Young Black Men Killed by US Police at Highest Rate in Year of 1,134 Deaths," *The Guardian*, December 31, 2015. *The Guardian's* database is available online (www.theguardian.com/us-news/ng-interactive/2015/jun/01/the-counted-police-killings-us-database#).

11. Kimberly Kindy, "Fatal Police Shootings in 2015 Approaching 400 Nationwide," *Washington Post*, May 30, 2015.

12. Kimberly Kindy and Kimbriell Kelly, "Thousands Dead, Few Prosecuted," *Washington Post*, April 11, 2015.

13. Ibid.

14. Ibid.

15. Kindy, "Fatal Police Shootings in 2015 Approaching 400 Nationwide."

16. "Policing: Don't Shoot," *The Economist*, December 13, 2014.

17. Final Report of the President's Task Force on 21st Century Policing, Washington D.C., May 2015. Action Item 2.2.4., p. 21.

18. Ibid.

19. 42 U.S.C. 14141.

20. "Investigation of the Ferguson Police Department," United States Department of Justice, Civil Rights Division. Washington, D.C., March 4, 2015. This report is heavily quoted in the following paragraphs.

21. "Policing: Don't Shoot," *The Economist*. This article cites Pew poll data. Among whites, 64 percent view the grand jury decision not to indict in the Michael Brown case as correct, but only 28 percent agree with the decision in the case of Eric Garner, suggesting a higher level of condemnation of the police behavior in that case, potentially attributable to the objective evidence available in the form of the video.

22. Diane Vaughan, *Controlling Unlawful Organizational Behavior: Social Structure and Corporate Misconduct* (University of Chicago Press, 1983), p. 55, summarizing observations by Robert K. Merton, in *Social Theory and Social Structure*, enlarged edition (New York: Free Press, 1968), pp. 185–214.

23. See chapter 12, "Performance-Enhancing Risks," in Malcolm K. Sparrow, *The Character of Harms: Operational Challenges in Control* (Cambridge University Press, 2008).

24. J. Q. Wilson and G. Kelling, "Broken Windows: The Police and Neighborhood Safety," *Atlantic Monthly* (March 1982), pp. 29–38.

25. Bruce Western, "The Man Who Foresaw Baltimore," *Politico Magazine*, April 30, 2015.

26. "Don't Shoot," *The Economist*. (www.economist.com/news/united-states/21636044-americas-police-kill-too-many-people-some-forces-are-showing-how-smarter-less).

27. Kevin Williams, Wesley Lowery, and Mark Berman, "University of Cincinnati Police Officer Who Shot Man during Traffic Stop Charged with Murder," *Washington Post*, July 29, 2015.

28. See the university's FAQ sheet on the police department (www.uc.edu/news/NR.aspx?id=22004).

29. "Policing: Don't Shoot," *The Economist*.

30. David H. Bayley, Michael A. Davis, and Ronald L. Davis, "Race and Policing: An Agenda for Action," *New Perspectives in Policing Bulletin* (Washington, D.C.: U.S. Department of Justice, National Institute of Justice, 2015), NCJ 248624, p. 1.

31. Anthony A. Braga and Rod K. Brunson, "The Police and Public Discourse on 'Black on Black' Violence," *New Perspectives in Policing Bulletin*, (Washington, D.C.: U.S. Department of Justice, National Institute of Justice), 2015, NCJ 248588.

32. A listing can be found at http://en.wikipedia.org/wiki/List_of_killings_by_law_enforcement_officers_in_the_United_Kingdom.

33. A listing can be found at http://en.wikipedia.org/wiki/List_of_killings_by_law_enforcement_officers_in_Canada.

34. Jamiles Lartney, "By the Numbers: U.S. Police Kill More in Days than Other Countries do in Years," *The Guardian*, June 9, 2015.

35. Jon Swaine, "The Counted: Number of People Killed by Police This Year Reaches 500," *The Guardian*, June 10, 2015.

36. The special significance of chases and their connection with beatings is noted by Couper, *Arrested Development*, footnote 15, pp. 33–34.

37. Jason Kandel and Tony Shin, "Sheriff Orders Immediate Internal Investigation into Arrest," seen on "Disturbing Video," *NBC4 News*, Southern California. Friday, April 10, 2015. Within two weeks the San Bernardino County's Board of Supervisors approved a settlement with the victim for $650,000. The officers' use of force remains under investigation (www.nbclosangeles.com/news/local/Man-on-Stolen-Horse-Stunned-by-Sheriffs-Deputies-in-IE-299250951.html). See also Emma Lacey-Bordeaux, "Man Gets Huge Settlement after Televised Police Beating" (http://edition.cnn.com/2015/04/22/us/california-horseback-beating-settlement/index.html?iref=obinsite).

38. David C. Couper, *Arrested Development: A Veteran Police Chief*

Sounds Off about Protest, Racism, Corruption, and the Seven Steps Necessary to Improve Our Nation's Police (Indianapolis, Ind.: Dog Ear Publishing: 2011), pp. 33–34.

39. Couper, *Arrested Development*, footnote 15, pp. 33–34.

40. Kindy, "Fatal Police Shootings in 2015 Approaching 400 Nationwide."

41. Christopher Cooper, "Entrenched Subculture Is at Root of Police Brutality and Bias Cases," op-ed, *Philadelphia Inquirer*, July 21, 2000. This article is cited in David Couper's *Arrested Development*, p. 29.

42. Ibid.

43. Charles Ramsey, "The Challenge of Policing in a Democratic Society: A Personal Journey toward Understanding," *New Perspectives in Policing Bulletin* (Washington, D.C.: U.S. Department of Justice, National Institute of Justice, 2014), NCJ 245992, p. 10.

44. Couper, *Arrested Development*, p. 16.

45. Ramsey, "The Challenge of Policing in a Democratic Society: A Personal Journey toward Understanding," *New Perspectives in Policing Bulletin* (Washington, D.C.: U.S. Department of Justice, National Institute of Justice, 2014), NCJ 245992, pp. 10–11.

46. Anthony A. Braga, "Crime Control Revisited," *New Perspectives in Policing Bulletin* (Washington, D.C.: U.S. Department of Justice, National Institute of Justice, 2015, forthcoming).

Chapter 2

1. *Measuring What Matters: Proceedings from the Policing Research Institute Meetings,* edited by Robert H. Langworthy. Research Report (Washington, D.C.: U.S. Department of Justice, National Institute of Justice, July 1999), NCJ 170610 (www.ncjrs.gov/pdffiles1/nij/170610.pdf).

2. Mark H. Moore and others, *Recognizing Value in Policing: The Challenge of Measuring Police Performance* (Washington, D.C.: Police Executive Research Forum, 2002).

3. Mark H. Moore and Anthony Braga, *The "Bottom Line" of Policing: What Citizens Should Value (and Measure!) in Police Performance* (Washington, D.C.: Police Executive Research Forum, 2003) (www.policeforum. org/assets/docs/Free_Online_Documents/Police_Evaluation/the%20 bottom%20line%20of%20policing%202003.pdf).

4. Wesley G. Skogan, "Measuring What Matters: Crime, Disorder, and Fear," in *Measuring What Matters: Proceedings from the Policing Research Institute Meetings,* edited by Robert H. Langworthy. Research Report (Washington, D.C.: U.S. Department of Justice, National Institute of Justice, July 1999), NCJ 170610 (www.ncjrs.gov/pdffiles1/nij/170610.pdf), pp. 36–53, at 38.

5. For a detailed study of the frequency with which various forms of victimization are not reported to the police, see Lynn Langton and others, *Victimizations Not Reported to the Police, 2006–2010.* Special Report (Wash-

ington, D.C.: U.S. Department of Justice, Bureau of Justice Statistics, August 2012), NCJ 238536 (www.bjs.gov/content/pub/pdf/vnrp0610.pdf).

6. For a detailed discussion of invisible harms and the special challenges involved in controlling them, see chapter 8, "Invisible Harms," in Malcolm K. Sparrow, *The Character of Harms: Operational Challenges in Control* (Cambridge University Press, 2008).

7. Sparrow, *The Character of Harms*, pp. 143–44

8. Adapted from Malcolm K. Sparrow, "Foreword," in *Financial Supervision in the 21st Century*, edited by A. Joanne Kellerman, Jakob de Haan, and Femke de Vries (New York: Springer-Verlag, 2013). This framework was first described in Sparrow in "The Sabotage of Harms: An Emerging Art Form for Public Managers," ESADE Institute of Public Governance and Management, E-newsletter (March 2012).

9. The report, which is not public, was provided to the author by Assistant Commissioner Wilhelmy.

10. The advent of the six-axis or "full-flight" simulators for pilot training in the 1990s is regarded as one of the most significant recent contributors to enhanced safety in commercial aviation.

11. Carl B. Klockars, "Some Really Cheap Ways of Measuring What Really Matters," in *Measuring What Matters: Proceedings from the Policing Research Institute Meetings*, edited by Robert H. Langworthy. Research Report (Washington, D.C.: U.S. Department of Justice, National Institute of Justice, July 1999), NCJ 170610 (www.ncjrs.gov/pdffiles1/nij/170610.pdf), pp. 195–214, at 197.

12. See, for example, Herman Goldstein, *Policing a Free Society* (Cambridge, Mass.: Ballinger, 1977).

13. See, for example, Moore and Braga, *The "Bottom Line" of Policing*, and Moore and others, *Recognizing Value in Policing*.

14. See, for example, Robert D. Behn, "Why Measure Performance? Different Purposes Require Different Measures," *Public Administration Review* 63, no. 5 (September/October 2003), pp. 586–606.

15. See, for example, Sparrow, *The Character of Harms*.

16. Goldstein, *Policing a Free Society*, p. 35.

17. Robert D. Behn, "On the Core Drivers of CitiStat: It's not Just about the Meetings and the Maps," *Bob Behn's Public Management Report* 2, no. 3 (November 2004).

18. Mark H. Moore and Margaret Poethig, "The Police as an Agency of Municipal Government: Implications for Measuring Police Effectiveness," in *Measuring What Matters: Proceedings from the Policing Research Institute Meetings*, edited by Robert H. Langworthy. Research Report (Washington, D.C.: U.S. Department of Justice, National Institute of Justice, July 1999), NCJ 170610 (www.ncjrs.gov/pdffiles1/nij/170610.pdf), pp. 151–67, at 153.

19. Ibid., p.157.

20. Moore and others, *Recognizing Value in Policing*, p. 76, table 2.

21. William J. Bratton, "Great Expectations: How Higher Expectations

for Police Departments Can Lead to a Decrease in Crime," in *Measuring What Matters: Proceedings from the Policing Research Institute Meetings,* edited by Robert H. Langworthy. Research Report (Washington, D.C.: U.S. Department of Justice, National Institute of Justice, July 1999), NCJ 170610 (www.ncjrs.gov/pdffiles1/nij/170610.pdf), pp. 11–26, at 15.

22. Moore and others, *Recognizing Value in Policing,* pp. 24–25.

23. Ibid., p. 25.

24. G. Kelling, "Measuring What Matters: A New Way of Thinking about Crime and Public Order," in *Measuring What Matters: Proceedings from the Policing Research Institute Meetings,* edited by Robert H. Langworthy. Research Report (Washington, D.C.: U.S. Department of Justice, National Institute of Justice), July 1999, NCJ 170610 (www.ncjrs.gov/pdffiles1/nij/170610.pdf), pp. 27–35, at 27.

25. Klockars, "Some Really Cheap Ways of Measuring What Really Matters," pp. 205–08, at 206.

26. Stuart A. Scheingold, "Constituent Expectations of the Police and Police Expectations of Constituents," in *Measuring What Matters: Proceedings from the Policing Research Institute Meetings,* edited by Robert H. Langworthy. Research Report (Washington, D.C.: U.S. Department of Justice, National Institute of Justice, July 1999), NCJ 170610 (https://www.ncjrs.gov/pdffiles1/nij/170610.pdf), pp. 183–92, at 186.

27. Wesley G. Skogan, *Disorder and Decline: Crime and the Spiral of Decay in American Neighborhoods* (New York: Free Press, 1990), p. 166.

28. Ibid., p. 172.

29. Moore and others, *Recognizing Value in Policing.*

30. Ibid., p. 79.

31. Behn, "Why Measure Performance?"

32. For a summary of this analysis, see Ibid., p. 593, table 2.

33. Sparrow, *The Character of Harms,* pp. 123–24. See chapter 6, "Puzzles of Measurement," for a discussion of the unique characteristics of a risk-control performance account.

34. The formal structure and essential rigors of the problem-oriented approach are described in detail in Sparrow, *The Character of Harms,* chapter 7. The associated performance measurement challenges are explored in chapters 5 and 6.

35. For a detailed discussion of the potential tensions between problem-oriented policing and "evidence-based" program evaluation techniques, see Malcolm K. Sparrow, "Governing Science," *New Perspectives in Policing Bulletin* (Washington, D.C.: U.S. Department of Justice, National Institute of Justice, 2011). Also chapter 4 here.

36. See, for example, Melissa Hipolit, "Former Police Officer Exposes Chesterfield's Ticket Quota Goals," *CBS6 Noon News,* July 14, 2014 (http://wtvr.com/2014/07/14/chesterfield-quota-investigation).

37. "Whew! No More Traffic Ticket Quotas in Illinois," *CNBC News, Law Section,* June 16, 2014 (www.cnbc.com/id/101762636#).

38. Andrew P. Scipione, "Foreword," in John A. Eterno and Eli B. Silverman, *The Crime Numbers Game: Management by Manipulation* (Boca Raton, Fla.: CRC Press, 2012), p. xviii.

39. Klockars, "Some Really Cheap Ways of Measuring What Really Matters," p. 196.

40. Ibid.

41. Moore and others, *Recognizing Value in Policing*, pp. 42–43.

42. Ibid., p. 38.

43. Moore and Braga, *The "Bottom Line" of Policing*, p. 37

44. Langton and others, *Victimizations not Reported to the Police, 2006– 2010*, p. 5.

45. Ibid.

46. See note 6.

47. Eterno and Silverman, *The Crime Numbers Game*, pp. 85–104.

48. Wesley G. Skogan, *Police and Community in Chicago: A Tale of Three Cities* (Oxford University Press, 2006). Chapter 3 describes crime-recording practices used by Chicago police during the 1980s.

49. Skogan, "Measuring What Matters: Crime, Disorder, and Fear," p. 38.

50. See the discussion of alleged manipulation of crime statistics by the NYPD below, under "Integrity Issues Related to CompStat and Crime Reporting at the NYPD."

51. Eterno and Silverman, *The Crime Numbers Game,* pp. 11–12.

52. Kevin Rawlinson, "Police Crime Figures Being Manipulated, Admits Chief Inspector," *Guardian* (December 18, 2013).

53. Ibid.

54. David Bernstein, and Noah Isackson, "The Truth about Chicago's Crime Rates," *Chicago Magazine*, Special Report, Part 1: April 7, 2014; Part 2: May 19, 2014.

55. Paul Hutcheon, "Independent Watchdog Refuses to Endorse Police Statistics That Claim Crime Is at a Near 40-Year Low," *Sunday Herald*, August 17, 2014.

56. Eterno and Silverman, *The Crime Numbers Game,* pp. 9–12.

57. Donald T. Campbell, *Assessing the Impact of Planned Social Change.* Occasional Paper Series, #8 (Hanover, N.H.: Dartmouth College, Public Affairs Center, December 1976), p. 49, cited in Eterno and Silverman, *The Crime Numbers Game,* p. 10.

58. Campbell, *Assessing the Impact of Planned Social Change*, pp. 50–51.

59. Diana Vaughan, *Controlling Unlawful Organizational Behavior: Social Structure and Corporate Misconduct* (University of Chicago Press, 1983), p. 55, summarizing observations by Robert K. Merton in Robert K. Merton, *Social Theory and Social Structure,* enlarged ed. (New York: Free Press, 1968), pp. 185–214.

60. For a detailed discussion of this phenomenon, see chapter 12, "Performance-Enhancing Risks," in Sparrow, *The Character of Harms.*

61. Robert Zink, "The Trouble with CompStat," *PBA Magazine* (Summer 2004), cited in Eterno and Silverman, *The Crime Numbers Game*, p. 27.

62. Part 1 Index Crimes, as defined under the Uniform Crime Reporting system, are aggravated assault, forcible rape, murder, robbery, arson, burglary, larceny-theft, and motor vehicle theft.

63. Bernstein and Isackson, "The Truth about Chicago's Crime Rates," Part I.

64. Bratton, "Great Expectations," p. 15.

65. Moore and others, *Recognizing Value in Policing*, p. 150.

66. Eterno and Silverman, *The Crime Numbers Game*, pp. 28–34.

67. Bratton, "Crime by the Numbers," *New York Times*, op-ed, February 17, 2010.

68. Ibid.

69. Ibid.

70. Graham Rayman, "The NYPD Tapes: Inside Bed-Stuy's 81st Precinct," *Village Voice*, May 4, 2010; Rayman, "The NYPD Tapes, Part 2: Ghost Town," *Village Voice*, May 11, 2010; Rayman, "The NYPD Tapes, Part 3: A Detective Comes Forward about Downgraded Sexual Assaults," *Village Voice*, June 8, 2010; Rayman, "The NYPD Tapes, Part 4: The Whistle Blower, Adrian Schoolcraft," *Village Voice*, June 15, 2010; Rayman, "The NYPD Tapes, Part 5: The Corroboration," *Village Voice*, August 25, 2010; Rayman, "The NYPD Tapes Confirmed," *Village Voice*, March 7, 2012. The entire series of articles is available online (www.villagevoice.com/special-Reports/the-nypd-tapes-the-village-voices-series-on-adrian-schoolcraft-by-graham-rayman-4393217/).

71. William K. Rashbaum, "Retired Officers Raise Questions on Crime Data," *New York Times*, February 6, 2010.

72. Al Baker and Ray Rivera, "5 Officers Face Charges in Fudging of Statistics," *New York Times,* October 15, 2010.

73. Al Baker and William K. Rashbaum, "New York City to Examine Reliability of Its Crime Reports," *New York Times*, January 5, 2011.

74. David N. Kelley and Sharon L McCarthy, "The Report of the Crime Reporting Review Committee to Commissioner Raymond W. Kelly Concerning CompStat Auditing," April 8, 2013. This report is heavily quoted in the following paragraphs.

75. Skogan, "Measuring What Matters: Crime, Disorder, and Fear."

76. Ibid., p. 38.

77. Kelley and McCarthy, "CompStat Auditing Report," p. 54.

78. For a thorough analysis of this issue, see chapter 4, "Distinguishing CompStat's Effects," in Robert D. Behn, *The PerformanceStat Potential: A Leadership Strategy for Producing Results* (Brookings Institution Press, 2014). Behn, who is a great admirer of *PerformanceStat* systems in general, surveys the literature on the subject, considers the ten other explanations most commonly put forward as alternative explanations, and concludes that due to the limitations of the methods of social science, we will probably never know for

sure what proportion of the crime reductions seen from 1994 onward was due to CompStat and what proportion is attributable to other factors.

79. Kelley and McCarthy, "CompStat Auditing Report," p. 21.

80. *Measuring What Matters: Proceedings from the Policing Research Institute Meetings,* edited by Robert H. Langworthy. Research Report (Washington, D.C.: U.S. Department of Justice, National Institute of Justice, July 1999), NCJ 170610 (www.ncjrs.gov/pdffiles1/nij/170610.pdf).

81. See, for example, Herman Goldstein, "Improving Policing: A Problem-Oriented Approach," *Crime and Delinquency* 25 (April 1979), pp. 236–58.

82. See, for example, Goldstein, "Improving Policing: A Problem-Oriented Approach," and Goldstein, *Policing a Free Society.*

83. See, for example, Moore and Braga, *The "Bottom Line" of Policing*, and Moore and others, *Recognizing Value in Policing.*

Chapter 3

1. "Investigation of the Ferguson Police Department," United States Department of Justice, Civil Rights Division, Washington, D.C., March 4, 2015, p. 87.

2. Ibid.

3. Anthony A. Braga, "Crime and Policing Revisited," *New Perspectives in Policing Bulletin* (Washington, D.C.: U.S. Department of Justice, National Institute of Justice, 2015), NCJ 248888.

4. Ibid., p. 17.

5. Ibid., p. 2.

6. Ronald V. Clarke, *Situational Crime Prevention: Successful Case Studies* (New York: Harrow and Heston, 1992), p. 4, as quoted in Malcolm K. Sparrow, *The Regulatory Craft* (Brookings Institution Press, 2000), pp. 219–20.

7. Herman Goldstein, "Address to the Summer Conference of the Association of Chief Police Officers (ACPO)," p. 7, as quoted in Sparrow, *The Regulatory Craft*, p. 220.

8. U.K. National Crime Information Service, "The National Intelligence Model" (2000), p. 14.

9. David Alan Sklansky, "The Persistent Pull of Police Professionalism," *New Perspectives in Policing* (National Institute of Justice and Harvard Kennedy School, March 2011), p. 8.

10. Predictive analytics software and services are sold by IBM, SAS, and SAP, among others.

11. Sklansky, "The Persistent Pull of Professionalism," pp. 8–9.

12. Ibid., p. 9. Drawing on Peter K. Manning, *The Technology of Policing: Crime Mapping, Information Technology, and the Rationality of Crime Control* (New York University Press, 2008), p. 252,

13. Final Report of the President's Task Force on 21st Century Policing, Washington, D.C., May 2015, p. 43.

14. David C. Couper, *Arrested Development: A Veteran Police Chief Sounds*

Off about Protest, Racism, Corruption, and the Seven Steps Necessary to Improve Our Nation's Police (Indianapolis, Ind.: Dog Ear Publishing, 2011), p. 13.

15. Sklansky, "The Persistent Pull of Police Professionalism," p. 7.

16. Charles Ramsey, "The Challenge of Policing in a Democratic Society: A Personal Journey toward Understanding," *New Perspectives in Policing Bulletin* (Washington, D.C.: U.S. Department of Justice, National Institute of Justice, 2014), NCJ 245992, p. 5.

17. A. A. Braga, B. C. Welsh, and C. Schnell, "Can Policing Disorder Reduce Crime? A Systematic Review and Meta-Analysis," *Journal of Research in Crime and Delinquency* 52 (2015), especially p. 22.

18. Sklansky, "The Persistent Pull of Police Professionalism," p. 11.

19. Ibid., p. 13.

20. Braga, "Crime and Policing Revisited," p. 18. Citing H. Goldstein, "Improving Policing: A Problem-Oriented Approach," *Crime and Delinquency* 25 (1979), pp. 236–58. See also H. Goldstein, *Problem-Oriented Policing* (Temple University Press, 1990).

21. Adrian Leigh, Tim Read, and Nick Tilley, "Problem-Oriented Policing," Paper 75, p. 39, Crime Detection and Prevention series (Police Research Group, Home Office, London, 1996). Cited in Malcolm K. Sparrow, *The Regulatory Craft*, pp. 209–10.

22. Sparrow, *The Regulatory Craft*, pp. 208–09.

23. Herman Goldstein, Address to the Summer Conference of the Association of Chief Police Officers (ACPO), p. 3.

24. Herman Goldstein, *Problem-Oriented Policing* (New York: Mc-Graw-Hill, 1990), pp. 34–35, 66–8.

25. Malcolm K. Sparrow, *The Character of Harms: Operational Challenges in Control* (Cambridge University Press, 2008), pp. 94–95.

26. Ibid., p. 119.

27. Ibid., pp. 143–44.

28. The elements in the left-hand column of table 3-1 have been adapted from an analysis of the organizational capabilities prescribed under the heading "Safety Management Systems" in civil aviation. For details, see Malcolm K. Sparrow (principal author), Edward W. Stimpson (chair), J. Randolph Babbitt, William O. McCabe, and Carl W. Vogt, *Managing Risks in Civil Aviation: A Review of the FAA's Approach to Safety*, report of the Independent Review Team Blue Ribbon panel appointed by Secretary of Transportation Mary E. Peters (Washington, D.C.: September 2, 2008), p. 48.

29. Herman Goldstein, "On Further Developing Problem-Oriented Policing: The Most Critical Need, the Major Impediments, and a Proposal," *Crime Prevention Studies* 15 (2003).

Chapter 4

1. Lawrence W. Sherman, *Ideas in American Policing: Evidence-Based Policing* (Washington, D.C.: Police Foundation, July 1998), p. 3.

2. Ibid., pp. 3–4.

3. Charles E. Lindblom, *Inquiry and Change: The Troubled Attempts to Understand and Shape Society* (Yale University Press, 1990), p. vii.

4. Ibid., p. 11.

5. Mark H. Moore, "Improving Police through Expertise, Experience, and Experiments," in *Police Innovation: Contrasting Perspectives*, edited by David Weisburd and Anthony Braga (Cambridge University Press, 2006), p. 325.

6. Mark H. Moore, "Learning While Doing: Linking Knowledge to Policy in the Development of Community Policing and Violence Prevention in the United States," in *Integrating Crime Prevention Strategies: Propensity and Opportunity*, edited by Per-Olof H. Wikstrom and others (Stockholm: National Council of Crime Prevention, 1995), pp. 301–31.

7. Ibid., pp. 302–03.

8. Ibid., p. 310.

9. Malcolm K. Sparrow, *The Character of Harms: Operational Challenges in Control* (Cambridge University Press, 2008), pp. 8–9.

10. Moore, "Learning While Doing," p. 307.

11. For this purpose, single group pretest/posttest designs are perfectly adequate, whereas these are regarded as "inadequate and uninterpretable" by the experimentalists. See "Standards of Evaluations in Problem-Oriented Policing Projects: Good Enough?" in *Evaluating Crime Reduction Initiatives*, edited by Johannes Knutsson and Nick Tilley, Crime Prevention Studies (book series), vol. 24 (Monsey, N.Y.: Criminal Justice Press, 2009), pp. 21, 23.

12. John E. Eck, "Learning from Experience in Problem-Oriented Policing and Situational Prevention: The Positive Functions of Weak Evaluations and the Negative Functions of Strong Ones," in *Evaluation of Crime Prevention*, edited by Nick Tilley, Crime Prevention Studies, vol. 14 (Monsey, N.Y.: Criminal Justice Press, 2002), p. 109.

13. For a detailed exploration of the differences between functions, processes, and problems and the implications for agency operations, see chapter 2, "A Different Type of Work," in Sparrow, *The Character of Harms*, pp. 47–72.

14. I refer to this elsewhere as the whack-a-mole model for risk-control operations; see Sparrow, *The Character of Harms*, pp. 143–46.

15. Nick Tilley points out that, in asking "what works," the *what* can refer to particular interventions, classes of interventions, mechanisms, strategies, or other more complex combinations of the four. He stresses the need to be clear about which level of object one is evaluating. See Nick Tilley, "What's the 'What' in 'What Works?' Health, Policing, and Crime Prevention," in *Evaluating Crime Reduction Initiatives*, edited by Johannes Knutsson and Nick Tilley, pp. 121–45.

16. Anthony A. Braga and Brenda J. Bond, "Policing Crime and Disorder Hot Spots: A Randomized Controlled Trial," *Criminology* 46, no. 3 (2008), p. 585.

17. David Weisburd and others, "Is Problem-Oriented Policing Effective in Reducing Crime and Disorder? Findings from a Campbell Systematic Review," *Criminology and Public Policy* 9, no. 1 (2010), pp. 139–72.

18. Such reviews follow the protocols of the Campbell Collaboration and focus on experimental and quasi-experimental studies. See www.campbellcollaboration.org/.

19. Weisburd and others, "Is Problem-Oriented Policing Effective," p. 153.

20. Vote counting essentially grants one vote to each study incorporated into a meta-analysis. Tallying the votes provides an overall score indicating whether a specific intervention produces positive outcomes more often than not, according to the compiled evidence. It is generally regarded as an unsophisticated approach because it makes no corrections for the relative sizes and quality of the different experiments. However, when researchers aim to combine the results from several studies involving different interventions (as is the case with Weisburd's Campbell Review), any of the more sophisticated statistical techniques for combining outcomes might be regarded as mathematically inappropriate, and vote counting might seem more reasonable in these circumstances.

21. Weisburd and others, "Is Problem-Oriented Policing Effective," p. 153.

22. Ibid., p. 159.

23. Ibid., p. 164.

24. Ray Pawson and Nick Tilley, *Realistic Evaluation* (London: Sage Publications, 1997), p. 50. For a discussion of growing dissatisfaction among scholars with prevailing approaches to evaluation and evidence—spanning medicine, education, early childhood programs, and international development, see Katya Fels Smyth and Lisbeth B. Schorr, "A Lot to Lose: A Call to Rethink What Constitutes 'Evidence' in Finding Social Interventions That Work," Working Paper series (Cambridge, Mass.: Malcolm Weiner Center for Social Policy, Harvard University Kennedy School of Government, January 2009) (http://108.174.148.9/~lisbeths/wp-content/uploads/2015/02/Alottolosejan2009.pdf)

25. Weisburd and others, "Is Problem-Oriented Policing Effective," p. 140.

26. Ibid., p. 164. An earlier study by Weisburd and Eck, designed to test the efficacy of various policing strategies, drew the same essential conclusion: "The authors find that many policing practices applied broadly throughout the United States either have not been the subject of systematic research or have been examined in the context of research designs that do not allow practitioners or policy makers to draw very strong conclusions," p. 42. See David Weisburd and John E. Eck, "What Can Police Do to Reduce Crime, Disorder, and Fear?" *Annals of the American Academy of Political and Social Sciences* 593 (May 2004), pp. 42–65.

27. Gilles Paquet, *Crippling Epistemologies and Governance Failures: A Plea for Experimentalism* (University of Ottawa Press, 2009), p. xv.

28. Nearby residents might have intervened if they had known what was happening.

29. Braga and Bond, "Policing Crime," pp. 577–607.

30. Ibid., p. 598.

31. Ibid., p. 599.

32. For a detailed discussion of the dimensionality of problems and the implications for control strategies, see chapter 4, "Defining Problems: Picking the Dimensions," in Sparrow, *The Character of Harms*, pp. 93–100.

33. Weisburd and others, "Is Problem-Oriented Policing Effective," p. 147. The study also located six quasi-experimental designs, and four of these were also place-based. The remaining two quasi-experiments focused on probationers and parolees, respectively, who are presumably more easily subjected to experimental manipulation than other segments of the public.

34. Paquet, *Crippling Epistemologies*, p. xvii.

35. Pawson and Tilley, *Realistic Evaluation*, p. 57.

36. Discussion at Harvard Law School, moderated by Professor Philip Heymann and Mathea Falco, January 30, 2009.

37. Ernest Nagel, *The Structure of Science* (New York: Harcourt, Brace and World, 1961), p. 5. Quoted in Lindblom, *Inquiry and Change*, pp. 161–62.

38. Lindblom, *Inquiry and Change*, p. 137.

39. The term *randomistas* appeared first in the field of international development economics, where it applies to those who consider randomized controlled trials (RCT) to be the gold standard when it comes to determining intervention effects.

40. This approach stems from the work of Cook and Campbell in 1979. See T. D. Cook and D. T. Campbell, *Quasi-Experimentation: Design and Analysis Issues for Field Settings* (Chicago: Rand-McNally, 1979). In 1998, a formal scale, now known as the *Maryland Scientific Methods Scale*, was laid out in L. W. Sherman and others, *Preventing Crime: What Works, What Doesn't, What's Promising*, Research in Brief (Washington, D.C.: National Institute of Justice, July 1998), NCJ 17176. A more recent version of the scale is laid out in Brandon C. Welsh, "Evidence-Based Crime Prevention: Scientific Basis, Trends, Results, and Implications for Canada," Research Report 2007-1 (Ottawa, Ont.: National Crime Prevention Centre, Public Safety, June 2007), pp. 13–14.

41. Welsh, "Evidence-Based Crime Prevention," p. 15.

42. Ibid., p. 5.

43. Jim Manzi observes that therapeutic biology "could often rely on the assumption of uniform biological response to generalize findings from randomized trials" but that "higher causal densities in social sciences" make such generalizations "hazardous." See Jim Manzi, "What Social Science Does—and Doesn't—Know," *City Journal* (Summer 2010) (www.city-journal.org/printable.php?id=6330).

44. In fact, the commercial sector seems to have figured out some ways to prevent the FDA from properly monitoring the trials. Most of the trials

are now conducted offshore, where the FDA cannot and does not supervise them. Roughly 80 percent of approved marketing applications for drugs and biologics contain data from foreign clinical trials, and more than half of clinical trial subjects were located overseas. The FDA inspects only 0.7 percent of foreign clinical trial sites. See Daniel Levinson, "Challenge to FDA's Ability to Monitor and Inspect Foreign Clinical Trials," Report OEI-01-08-00510 (Washington: Office of Inspector General, Department of Health and Human Services, June 2010), p. ii.

45. Nick Black, "Evidence Based Policy: Proceed with Care," *British Medical Journal* 323 (August 4, 2001), p. 275.

46. The youth homicide rate involves victims ages twenty-four and younger, and the juvenile homicide rate involves victims ages seventeen and younger.

47. For a full account of the project, see David M. Kennedy, Anne M. Piehl, and Anthony A. Braga, "Youth Violence in Boston: Gun Markets, Serious Youth Offenders, and a Use-Reduction Strategy," *Law and Contemporary Problems* 59, no. 1 (Winter 1996), pp. 147–96. For a subsequent analysis of pre/post data and comparisons with the trajectory of youth homicide rates in other cities, see Anthony A. Braga and others, "Problem-Oriented Policing, Deterrence, and Youth Violence: An Evaluation of Boston's Operation Ceasefire," *Journal of Research in Crime and Delinquency* 38 (2001), pp. 195–225.

48. Christakis does use techniques from social network analysis, which arose first as a subdiscipline of social science. However, social science has no monopoly on the uses and applications of the core ideas from social network analysis. In fact, mathematicians had been studying networks, which they called "graphs," for several hundred years before social science began to realize their significance for the study of social phenomena.

49. Interview with Professor Christakis, reported in Elizabeth Gudrais, "Networked: Exploring the Weblike Structures That Underlie Everything from Friendship to Cellular Behavior," *Harvard Magazine* (May/June 2010), p. 50.

50. See, for example, "Articles Abstracted to the Thomson-Reuters and Scopus Databases, 2007," *World Social Science Report 2010,* Annex 1, which provides basic statistics on the productivity of the social sciences.

51. This is a crude proxy, of course, for the rate of use of various inquiry methods because the categorization of articles is based heavily on the field of study as well as the research methods used.

52. See, for example, David Weisburd and Peter Neyroud, "Police Science: Toward a New Paradigm," *New Perspectives in Policing* (National Institute of Justice and Harvard Kennedy School, January 2011), p. 11.

53. Ibid., p. 12.

54. Ibid., p. 1.

55. This cause was championed for many years by the International Association of Law Enforcement Intelligence Analysts (IALEIA).

56. For a discussion of the circumstances affecting the costs and benefits of strong and weak evaluations, see Eck, "Learning from Experience," pp. 93–117.

Chapter 5

1. The police departments in many state-run (that is, public) university systems have the same authority and training standards as public police, and are accountable to public officials. Police departments in many private university settings answer directly to university administrators and are not formally accountable to any public official.

2. David H. Bayley and Clifford D. Shearing, *The New Structure of Policing: Description, Conceptualization, and Research Agenda*, Monograph (Washington: U.S. Department of Justice, National Institute of Justice), NCJ 187083, July 2001, p. vii.

3. Ronald van Steden and Jaap de Waard, "Acting Like Chameleons: On the McDonaldization of Private Security," *Security Journal* 26 (2013), pp. 294–309. See table 1, which provides a country-by-country breakdown.

4. David A. Sklansky, "Private Policing and Human Rights," *Law and Ethics of Human Rights* 5, no.1 (2011), pp. 111–36, 114.

5. Chris Stein, "As Cities Lay Off Police, Frustrated Neighborhoods Turn to Private Cops," *Christian Science Monitor,* April 5, 2013.

6. Rick Sarre and Tim Prenzler, *Private Security and Public Interest: Exploring Private Security Trends and Directions for Reform in the New Era of Plural Policing,* Report (Canberra, ACT: Australian Research Council), LP 0669518, April 2011, pp. 5, 14.

7. Sklansky, "Private Policing and Human Rights," p. 116.

8. Adam White, *The Politics of Private Security: Regulation, Reform, and Re-Legitimation* (Basingstoke, U.K.: Palgrave Macmillan, 2010).

9. Ibid., pp. 181–82.

10. Margaret Thatcher was leader of the Conservative Party in the United Kingdom from 1975 to 1990 and prime minister from 1979 to 1990.

11. The "New Labour" philosophy was used as the British Labour Party's campaign platform from 1994 onward. With Tony Blair and Gordon Brown as prime ministers, the Labour Party held power from 1997 to 2010.

12. Szu Ping Chan and agencies, "Timeline: How G4S's Bungled Olympics Security Contract Unfolded," *Daily Telegraph,* May 21, 2014. Available online (www.telegraph.co.uk/finance/newsbysector/supportservices/10070425/Timeline-how-G4Ss-bungled-Olympics-security-contract-unfolded.html).

13. White, *The Politics of Private Security: Regulation, Reform and Re-Legitimation*, p. 182.

14. The Bureau of Labor Statistics projects the number of private security guards to grow by 19 percent from 1 million to 1.2 million by 2020. "Private Security Industry Poised for Highest Growth Rate in Nine

Years," *PRWeb*, March 14, 2012. Available online (www.prweb.com/re-leases/2012/3/prweb9277026.htm).

15. Elizabeth E. Joh, "The Forgotten Threat: Private Policing and the State," *Indiana Journal of Global Legal Studies* 13, no. 2 (2006), pp. 357–89, 377.

16. Ibid., p. 388.

17. Gary T. Marx, "The Interweaving of Public and Private Police Undercover Work," in *Private Policing*, edited by C. Shearing and P. Stenning (Sage Publications, 1987). Quotes attributed to S. Ghezzi, "A Private Network of Social Control: Insurance Investigation Units," *Social Problems* 30, no. 5 (1983), pp. 521–31.

18. Marx, "The Interweaving of Public and Private Police Undercover Work," p. 5.

19. See ibid., p. 5. For a comprehensive study of the legal and constitutional issues surrounding the conduct of private police, and various approaches to regulating their behavior, see David A. Sklansky, "The Private Police," *UCLA Law Review* 46, no. 4 (1999), pp. 1165–287, 1245–46.

20. Jelle van Buuren and Monica den Boer, *A Report on the Ethical Issues Raised by the Increasing Role of Private Security Professionals in Security Analysis and Provision* (Oslo: International Peace Research Institute, December 2009), p. 51, citing S. Schneider in "Privatizing Economic Crime Enforcement: Exploring the Role of Private Sector Investigative Agencies in Combating Money Laundering," *Policing and Society* 16, no. 3, pp. 285–312, 305.

21. Marx, "The Interweaving of Public and Private Police Undercover Work," at note 9.

22. van Buuren and den Boer, *A Report on the Ethical Issues Raised by the Increasing Role of Private Security Professionals in Security Analysis and Provision*, p. 51.

23. Joh, "The Forgotten Threat: Private Policing and the State," p. 388.

24. The same is true of the London Tube bombings in 2005.

25. U.S. National Advisory Committee on Criminal Justice Standards and Goals, *Report of the Task Force on Private Security* (Washington, D.C.: U.S. Department of Justice, 1976), p. 18.

26. Elizabeth E. Joh, "The Paradox of Private Policing," UC Davis Legal Studies Research Paper series, Research Paper 23 (University of California, Davis, School of Law, January 2009), p. 69.

27. Bayley and Shearing, *The New Structure of Policing: Description, Conceptualization, and Research Agenda*, p. vii.

28. Canadian discussion of the public–private interface has used terms such as "plural policing" and "the safety and security web" to describe collaborative contributions to a safe environment. See Law Commission of Canada, *In Search of Security: The Future of Policing in Canada* (Ottawa: Law Commission of Canada, 2013), p. xiii.

29. Bayley and Shearing, *The New Structure of Policing: Description, Conceptualization, and Research Agenda*, p. viii.

30. Sklansky provides a seminal discussion of the underlying legal issues. See David A. Sklansky, "The Private Police," *UCLA Law Review* 46, no. 4 (1999), pp. 1165–287, 1245–46. For a discussion of the role the language of human rights might play in discussions of private policing, see David A. Sklansky, "Private Policing and Human Rights," *Law and Ethics of Human Rights* 5, no. 1 (2011), pp. 111–36.

31. van Buuren and den Boer, *A Report on the Ethical Issues Raised by the Increasing Role of Private Security Professionals in Security Analysis and Provision*, pp. 31–32.

32. A single pdf file containing all four hypotheticals is downloadable from the Program in Criminal Justice website (www.hks.harvard.edu/programs/criminaljustice/research-publications/executive-sessions/executive-session-on-policing-and-public-safety-2008-2014/publications).

33. Tim Ross, "Rush to Hire Private Companies for Public Policing 'Will Be Halted,'" *The Telegraph*, October 3, 2012.

34. For detailed analysis of the factors influencing privatization decisions, see John D. Donahue, *The Privatization Decision: Public Ends, Private Means* (New York: Basic Books, 1989). Also see Robert Waldersee and Michael Nest, "Corruption Risks in NSW Government Procurement: The Risk Management Challenge," *Keeping Good Companies* 64, no. 4 (May 2012), pp. 207–11. This list is the author's own compilation, derived from a variety of sources and discussions on public sector integrity and risk management.

35. Sharon Finegan, "Watching the Watchers: The Growing Privatization of Criminal Law Enforcement and the Need for Limits on Neighborhood Watch Associations," *University of Massachusetts Law Review* 8 (2013), p. 88.

36. Ibid., pp. 125, 130.

37. The Clery Act (1990) requires colleges and universities to publicly disclose campus crime rates on an annual basis, and specifies precisely which crime types must be reported.

38. The proportion of students offered admission who subsequently accept the offer.

39. Cramped conditions on long flights exacerbate the risk of deep-vein thrombosis.

40. Reputational concerns, for reputable airlines, act to some degree (and only in competitive markets) to realign public and private interests with respect to consumer protection issues.

41. Joh, "The Forgotten Threat: Private Policing and the State," p. 86.

42. Disagreements about means often arise because the university is inclined to provide a protective and somewhat permissive environment for students, and even tolerate or manage offending without recourse to law enforcement. University police can find themselves complicit in concealing offenses from the attention of public police agencies.

Chapter 6

1. John Alford and Richard Speed, "Client Focus in Regulatory Agencies," *Public Management Review* 8 (2006), pp. 313–31. Alford and Speed provide a careful examination of the ways in which a "client focus" needs to be adapted to be constructively applied within a regulatory setting. For a review of the application of customer-service ideals and business process improvement methods in reform of U.S. regulatory agencies, see chapters 4 and 5 in Malcolm K. Sparrow, *The Regulatory Craft: Controlling Risks, Solving Problems, and Managing Compliance* (Brookings Institution Press, 2000).

2. A one-week executive program titled "Strategic Management of Regulatory and Enforcement Agencies" was offered first at the Harvard Kennedy School in 1998 and is now offered twice a year. It also is offered twice a year in the Southern Hemisphere through the Australia and New Zealand School of Government.

3. J. E. Eck and E. B. Eck, "Crime Place and Pollution," *Criminology and Public Policy* 11 (2012), pp. 281–316. See also David Weisburd and others, "Is Problem-Oriented Policing Effective in Reducing Crime and Disorder? Findings from a Campbell Systematic Review," *Criminology and Public Policy* 9 (2010), pp. 139–72.

4. Ibid.

5. For a discussion of this class of risks and the special challenges they present to those responsible for control, see chapter 9, "Conscious Opponents," Malcolm K. Sparrow in *The Character of Harms: Operational Challenges in Control* (Cambridge University Press, 2008).

6. *Social* regulation, which centers on issues of health, safety, and welfare, usually is distinguished from *economic* regulation, which focuses on the healthy functioning of markets. Agencies of social regulation are given industrywide responsibility for the control of a specific category of risks or threats (for example, environmental, occupational safety, labor practices, and consumer product safety). By contrast, agencies of economic regulation seek to preserve competition, efficient market function, and fair trade practices within one specific industry (for example, transportation, utilities, communications, or financial services).

7. Martinez and others explored the potential application of "co-regulation" in food safety in both the United Kingdom and the United States. Co-regulation is described as involving "public and private sectors working hand-in-hand to deliver safer food at lower (regulatory) cost." See Marian Garcia Martinez and others, "Co-regulation as a Possible Model for Food Safety Governance: Opportunities for Public-Private Partnerships," *Food Policy* 32 (2007), pp. 299–314.

8. For an extensive catalogue of regulatory methods, see Arie Frieburg, *The Tools of Regulation* (Sydney: Federation Press, 2010).

9. For a broader regulatory view of the notion of co-production, see chapter 3, "Legal Compliance, Regulation, and Co-Production," in John Alford, *Engaging Public Sector Clients: From Service-Delivery to Co-Production* (Basingstoke, U.K.: Palgrave Macmillan, 2009).

10. For one of his best-known earlier works, see Herman Goldstein, "Improving Policing: A Problem-Oriented Approach," *Crime and Delinquency* 25 (1979), pp. 236–58. His most comprehensive treatise on problem-oriented policing is presented in Herman Goldstein, *Problem-Oriented Policing* (New York: McGraw-Hill, 1990).

11. For a detailed discussion of the varying dimensionality of harms/problems and the implications for control strategies, see chapter 4 in Sparrow, *The Character of Harms: Operational Challenges in Control.*

12. For a discussion of the differences between natural science and social science inquiry methods, as well as the appropriate mixture of these that is required to support problem-oriented policing, see chapter 4, "Governing Science," here.

Index